HEIR TO A DREAM

HEIR TO A DREAM

Pete Maravich
and
Darrel Campbell

with
Frank Schroeder

Thomas Nelson Publishers
Nashville

Published in Nashville, Tennessee, by Thomas Nelson, Inc., and distributed in Canada by Lawson Falle, Ltd., Cambridge, Ontario.

Printed in the United States of America.

Scripture quotations are from THE NEW KING JAMES VER-SION. Copyright © 1979, 1980, 1982, Thomas Nelson, Inc., Publishers.

Library of Congress Cataloging-in-Publication Data

Maravich, Pete, 1948-
    Heir to a dream.

    1. Maravich, Pete, 1948-   .   2. Basketball
players—United States—Biography.   3. Fathers and
sons—United States—Case studies.   4. Sports—United
States—Religious aspects—Case studies.   I. Campbell,
Darrel.   II. Schroeder, Frank.   III. Title.
GV884.M3A3   1987   796.32'3'0924 [B]   87-22004
ISBN 0-8407-7609-8

    2 3 4 5 6 7 8 9 10 - 97 96 95 94 93 92 91 90 89 88 87

*This book is dedicated
to the memory of
my father and mother,
Press and Helen Maravich.
They taught me that
character never quits
and that, with patience and persistence,
dreams can be realized.*

Contents

BOOK FIVE—SHATTERED DREAMS

BOOK SIX—HEIR OF SALVATION

Acknowledgments

The authors would like to thank all who made the research of this book a possibility. We would like to thank our wives, Jackie Maravich and Pamela Campbell, for holding down the forts as we spent hours away from them.

We would like to thank Roberta Schroeder for her objectivity and patience.

We would also like to acknowledge the quality contribution to this book given to us by Press and Ronnie Maravich. Their attention to detail and colorful descriptions helped immeasurably.

We wish to thank Jaeson and Joshua Maravich and Casey Jack Campbell for their inspiration. We hope that someday their dreams will also become a reality.

Finally, to Bruce Nygren, Steve Hines, and the editorial staff at Thomas Nelson Publishers, we thank them for their commitment.

Foreword

When I was approached to tell my life story, at first I was apprehensive. Old wounds, now healed, would need to be reopened to reveal the truth about past choices. It meant dropping the guarded fortress I had built around myself.

I didn't want to write a book that would candy coat what I've experienced; instead, I wished to communicate my personal struggle to find the elusive inner peace and happiness that seemed impossible most of my life.

That wish may sound strange coming from "Pistol Pete." I've had all the things this life has to offer in the way of "happiness." I've had world fame, and my name is in the record books. I've had money, cars, and honorary admiral status in the Navy, just to name a few.

Despite all the material wealth and acclaim, however, I am able now to write this book only because I was finally rescued from my self-destructive tendencies. Without a doubt my life was spared several times in the past, such as the night I was beaten, had a gun placed to my mouth, and was told I was about to die. Or the night I drove across a bridge at 145 miles an hour, contemplating suicide.

As a child I chose a road I thought would bring me fame, fortune, success, and, ultimately, happiness. Basketball was my dream, a dream handed down to me from my father.

Press Maravich had a dream of what basketball and basketball players could become one day, and his greatest desire was to help me become the realization of his vision. He gave to me his years of knowledge and experience, as well as the ultimate gift—a life dedicated to helping me become the best basketball player I could possibly be.

To tell my life story is to tell my father's story, the two are so interwoven. My dad handed me his legacy, and because he did I am his *Heir to a Dream*.

HEIR TO A DREAM

BOOK ONE

THE DREAM

——— 1 ———

Press

Springfield, Massachusetts May 1, 1987

I had heard about this shrine for basketball legends since I was ten years old. My dad, Press, had spoken the names of the old-timers reverently, as though they were departed family members—Nat Holman, Dutch Denhert, the Original Celtics. And, of course, Dr. James A. Naismith, the man who had started the indoor game with the round ball and peach baskets. Now, gazing at Naismith's shrine, the Memorial Basketball Hall of Fame, I felt my stomach flutter and throat tighten. Today, the final scene of Dad's dream would unfold when I slipped the gold ring on my finger and stood in the hall of champions. How I wished he were by my side.

Just five years earlier, playing with the Celtics in nearby Boston, it seemed the dream had died after another afternoon of dribbling, passing, and shooting a basketball on a hardwood floor. The final horn had blown on a green and white intrasquad game. The team had looked good, and the guys were pumped up as we came into the Celtic locker room. I had played well, scoring thirty-eight points. Other players were whooping and laughing, but I had to force a smile.

I sat near my locker, as I had done hundreds of times down through the years, but something was different. As I tossed my steamy-hot basketball shoes toward the locker, I heard, "Great game, Pistol. Lookin' good." I felt some slaps on the back and grinned weakly.

I peeled the hot socks away from my sweaty legs and down off my feet. It was inspection time. Great . . . the ankles weren't

15

swollen. I unfastened my rubberized knee sleeve. No problems. I should have been ecstatic, but I wasn't. I could only think of my father, wondering if what I was about to do would destroy his life.

Nearly twenty-five years had passed since Dad had handed me his vision of winning a championship ring. He had always wanted me to play on a winning team and be recognized as the best in the world. But through all the record-breaking years in high school and at LSU, and despite being a three-time all-American, player-of-the-year, NCAA all-time leading scorer, and spending a decade in the pros, winning a championship had eluded me. I couldn't get that ring!

Then just last season, a midseason deal had brought me to the Boston Celtics. My dream was in reach! The NBA championship banners hung row-after-row from the rafters of Boston Garden, a constant reminder that I, as a Celtic, was finally a member of a championship dynasty—a "winner."

Unfortunately, the team had lost to Philadelphia in the playoffs, and for the first time in many seasons I had been a seldom-used substitute. The memory of riding the bench gnawed at me. I had felt like a caged animal.

But this was a new season, a time to start fresh. I walked to the shower. The steam and hot water relaxed me, but I could not drive the thoughts from my head. I closed my eyes as the water ran down my face. I had led all scorers the two games I had started for the Celtics last year, but there were many who didn't think I could play "Celtics ball." All summer I had sat by the phone waiting for the call, offering me a new contract. The call hadn't come, and I'd heard the Celtics were shopping for another guard.

I was snapped out of my mental solitude for a second by the sounds of the locker room. "Bring on Philly!" several guys cheered. So many years I'd played on losing teams where seldom there'd been any fun and optimism. What a tradition Boston had!

This is what my dad had wanted for me. But he would just have to understand my decision. I had managed to score nearly 16,000 points in pro basketball, but the NBA had worn me out physically. And worse than any physical ailments, along the way I had picked up an attitude that can ruin any athlete—the wrong kind of pride. There was no way I would be part of a team that won a world championship while I sat on the bench! No amount of discipline, no depth of passion for basketball, no dream of my dad's, or anything could make me do that!

I dried off and dressed. Slowly I dug through the locker and filled my gym bag with what now seemed to be the relics of my entire life. "Good game, Pete!" Dave Cowens said with a smile. I waved him on. I couldn't find the words to tell him or anybody that this was it; the "Pistol" had fired his last shot. The diamond ring would be on someone else's finger. What would Dad say when I told him that his dream, the dream that had become Pistol Pete, was dead?

Waiting to hear my name called at the Hall of Fame, I knew I had been wrong that day five years ago. Dad's dream had come true, even though I had run away from the game of basketball, a lonely and bitter man who could no longer seek his boyhood hopes. But to understand my pursuit of the vision, and to see how it nearly robbed me of everything, you must know something of my heritage. You must learn about my father, because he was the original dreamer.

The dream first eased into my father's young heart and mind on cold January mornings in Aliquippa, Pennsylvania. The huge gray steel mills puffed thick black smoke, as if they were working hard to keep warm. My father, Peter Maravich, strode down the railroad tracks, his leather shoes crunching into the snow. The stretch of steel took him within thirty feet of his parents' new home in Logstown. But if he let his imagination go, he felt that with his fast feet, he could speed right on through Pittsburgh. Like the biggest and fastest locomotives, he could race through that metropolis to the far-reaching cities beyond. *No one can catch me*, he thought. *I'll pull out of Logstown, pick up speed through Aliquippa, and storm through Pittsburgh. Then with my engine at full steam, I'll leave this steel town so far behind, all they'll have left of Peter Maravich is a memory!*

17

He mused about his vision of becoming a great professional athlete. *That'll be my ticket out of here*, he thought. *I'm not gonna work in these mills the rest of my life.*

The conglomeration of brick and mortar, furnaces and fire, represented the backbone of industrial America in 1927. To a kid growing up in the Northeast, it represented his life and his future.

Every ounce of food, every thread of his clothing was a result of a job at the Jones and Laughlin Mill. Every kid my dad knew had a father or brother who eked out a living in the mill, and everyone assumed that all the boys would follow their fathers into the same way of life. My dad considered all the different options he would have there: the tin mill, the rod mill, the open hearth, the carpenter shop.

My grandfather had also worked long and hard on the night shift at Jones and Laughlin. Under a shroud of darkness during the midnight to 8 a.m. shift, he was mysteriously killed in a locomotive accident. Dad was only two years old at the time. His family told him stories about his father, and as he listened Grandpa's death seemed senseless and was difficult to accept.

But his father's death was not the only family death Dad would have to come to grips with. Dad was the only survivor of ten children. During World War I, a great flu epidemic swept the Northeast and claimed the lives of his six sisters and three brothers. Thoughts of the mill and the town itself conjured up feelings of hurt and the loss of loved ones.

His stepfather, George Kosanovich, was a huge man, about 6'3" and over 260 pounds. George was the only dad he'd known, and he loved him very much. But loving his dad and agreeing with him were two distinctly different things. George's vision and my dad's dream were at odds, and their relationship was strained because of it.

George continually thought up clever schemes to educate his stepson. He could think of no better way than to give Dad artistic opportunities such as music lessons that might benefit the whole family. Music played an important part in the life of the Kosanoviches. George and his nephews spent many nights eating dinner, drinking wine, and singing songs of the old country. My dad's cousins were about the same size as my grandpa and were affectionately called "The Four Tons." The mighty quartet would belt out Serbian melodies all through the night.

When a traveling salesman made George a good deal on some banjo lessons, he couldn't pass up the opportunity for his stepson. One year of lessons and Dad would get to keep the banjo. It was a deal George couldn't let pass. A year of violin lessons and a year of harp lessons followed, despite my dad's protests.

A year of violin lessons was the last thing Dad needed in his life. It was bad enough he had to live with the name Peter, a sissy name in those days. He heard them all: Petey, Pete-Pete, Peter Peter Pumpkin Eater, and so on. To add "Peter, the Violin Player" would've ruined him for good with his peers if word got around.

To escape the tag of violin player, Dad walked a few miles out of his way, down the tracks, and across Logstown to avoid an encounter with a friend who just might spread the news all over their neighborhood.

One day, Dad's stepbrothers, Lawerence or "Lazo," and Bob, were playing cards in a little shack they had built. As they played they kept a lively conversation going; but on this day Lazo and Bob got fed up with Dad. No matter what subject they discussed, Dad presumed to be an expert. Whatever Lazo and Bob said, he refuted. Finally, Bob had taken all he could and lashed out at Dad. "Well, if you want to know anything about everything, just ask the Pittsburgh Press!" he shouted.

Dad loved the sound of the name the second he heard it. It was a great substitute for Peter. From that day he was known as Press Maravich.

2

DANIEL BOYS

To my dad, school meant spending time with buddies and making new friends. Of course, he learned the basics, mastering his reading, writing, and arithmetic; but friends were much more important to him.

He was admired by his pals because he could do just about anything when it came to sports. He played baseball, some football, lots of street hockey, and basketball. But what Dad did best was create excitement with new and different games for his buddies to play. For instance, recess was consumed with games such as, "Buck, Buck, How Many Fingers Up?" Or the guys competed in a ferocious game of mumblety–peg.

Games such as these bonded the Logstown youngsters together, creating the necessary friendships so desperately needed in a world full of hard knocks. Dad could deal with the steel mill and the violin lessons, as long as he had his friends and the constant challenge of a game or sport to help occupy his time.

Grade school also offered a great time of discovery for Dad. He and his pals decided they should chew snuff, since snuff was the sign of real manhood.

A good chew came in handy when the guys hopped a train to Pittsburgh to see the Pirates play a Saturday afternoon game. After all, when they arrived at Forbes Field to shake hands with the ballplayers, all the athletes had wads in their mouths; and Dad and the boys knew they would be in good company with their cheeks bulging.

One day Dad struck up a conversation with one of the Pirates as he warmed up for the game.

"I was born about a two-base hit from here," Dad boasted, as he spat a brown stream of tobacco juice. He pointed with pride toward his old house on Sarah Street.

His buddies were impressed at his boldness. He continued by bragging of how far they had traveled to see the Pirates play.

"You boys are hoppin' freight trains?" the player inquired with a wink.

"You know it! We've been going to New Castle a lot, and we're planning to go to Cleveland a few times to see the air races," Dad answered eagerly.

"Well, I wouldn't do it . . . can't play ball if you're cut in half." He turned and threw the ball, showing the power of his arm.

As the boys hopped a freight car back home, Dad's mind swirled with the dream of someday being a professional athlete. That would get him out of Logstown. That would show them all.

As the freight train crawled through Aliquippa, a buddy nudged Dad out of his reverie in time to jump off their huge, slow-moving taxi. They continued these journeys from the spring through summer. The one-day jaunts solidified Dad's dream of leaving Aliquippa to explore and pursue all that the world had to offer.

My dad was a natural leader. He was agile, a glib talker, and quick-witted. He may not have been the smartest in his class, but he could think on his feet—a gift that helped him succeed and ultimately saved his life. His mind always buzzed with new ideas and concepts. These characteristics, mixed with a generous amount of loyalty, gave Dad the personality that won friends in no time at all.

If Dad's friends weren't impressed with his abilities, they were quickly converted the day in seventh grade when Dad pulled off one of his best stunts. Almost every child has a grade school teacher he despises and one whom he loves. Dad was no exception. Mrs. Banks was the teacher he loved. A blizzard couldn't stop him from running the mile to school when Mrs. Banks became his teacher. She was young and beautiful, and he wasn't afraid to say he dearly loved her. But one love overruled even Mrs. Banks, and that was his love for chewing tobacco. In her class he was forced to choose what he cherished more—his snuff or his teacher. Mrs. Banks had many rules in her class, including one on no chewing.

Dad's decision was made in seconds; he could live without Mrs.

Banks. All the boys spit out their snuff at her request; all but Dad. He cleverly devised a technique to control his saliva. By storing the snuff in a deep corner of his mouth, he could hold the wad three to four hours without spitting. When it came time to spit, he generated a small amount of saliva, and dribbled the juice into the inkwell on the corner of his desk. *This is a cinch!* he thought, keeping his eye on Mrs. Banks.

The true test came later in the day during the spelling test. Dad secretly made several deposits in the inkwell when Mrs. Banks walked up and down the aisles between the desks, quietly reading the spelling words for the class. He wasn't intimidated at all by her presence. In fact he could hardly wait for her to come by his desk so he could smell the scent of her perfume.

As she drew near, he sat up straight and waited for the next spelling word. In a tone as smooth as silk she carefully enunciated the word *emancipation*. Dad was excited. He knew the spelling of *emancipation* quite well. In his best handwriting, he proudly penned the word on his tablet. At the same moment, Mrs. Banks's perfume hit his nose. She stopped and asked, "Peter?"

His heart leaped at the sound of her voice. Only Mrs. Banks made the name *Peter* sound worth having.

"Yes, Mrs. Banks?" he answered, knowing for sure she was about to compliment his well-practiced handwriting and correct spelling.

"What on earth has happened to your ink?" she asked, with a bewildered look.

Dad's heart sank as his eyes zipped to his inkwell. The ink had turned a mysterious light blue from the chemical reaction of saliva and snuff! Before he could answer, Mrs. Banks took the inkwell, dumped it out, and replaced it with fresh ink. He breathed a sigh of relief as a couple of his fellow snuff brothers suppressed their giggles. Mrs. Banks smiled at Dad, and he grinned back, his face flushed.

Oddly enough, Dad used the inkwell as a spittoon the entire year. Mrs. Banks never caught on, but merely expected the light blue ink compositions from Peter Maravich.

Dad's cleverness and ingenuity came in handy as his love for basketball grew. Shooting hoops became a ritual as the boys learned they had a knack for the little-known sport. They stumbled upon basketball when they read about its development by a man named Dr. James A. Naismith. As a staff member of the Young Men's Christian Association (YMCA) training school in Springfield, Massachusetts, Professor Naismith had wanted a new gymnasium sport. The end result was an odd game called basketball. The rules were simple enough: bounce the ball and throw it into the basket. Whoever does it the most times scores the most points and wins.

As the boys' interests grew, newspapers and word of mouth were also spreading the news of the uniquely American sport. Dad and his friends heard of the newly formed professional league that featured the best team in the country, the world champion Original Celtics. Great players like Johnny Beckman, Pete Barry, Joe Lapchick, Dutch Denhert—the inventor of the pivot play—and Nat Holman—perhaps the greatest set shooter of all time—became their idols. But hearing about the sport and playing it were two vastly different things. Basketball may have been a gymnasium sport for Professor Naismith and the Original Celtics, but few people had access to a gymnasium in Logstown, least of whom were a bunch of eleven- and twelve-year-old boys.

As usual, Dad didn't let that stop him. He liked the concept of the game and was determined to play. He figured out what they needed. A basket was the easy item: They found an old bushel basket, cut out the bottom, and hammered it to a light pole on the street corner not far from my dad's house. The ball presented more of a problem, but Dad wouldn't be denied. Like a drill instructor, he barked out the orders for materials. One boy was to fetch a can, another a rock, another some black electrical tape from his uncle's hardware store. Dad brought some copies of the *Pittsburgh Press* as his contribution to their homemade sphere. After the materials were gathered and laid on the sidewalk, Dad went to work. He took the can and dropped the rock inside. Next, he wrapped single sheets of newspaper around the can one after another until the ball of paper was approximately the correct size. Then he took the electrical tape and began to wrap the paper. As the boys watched impatiently, he slowly wound the ball with the sticky tape until every inch of the paper was covered. Dad stood up and, with a crude but accurate push, sent the ball into the basket for the inauguration of the goal and ball. There was no lovely swish, but rather an ugly thwack, then thud as the ball fell through the basket and onto the pavement below. Hardly music to the ears, but to my dad it was the most beautiful thing he'd heard since Mrs. Banks first spoke his name.

The ugly black ball had no bounce, but the inability to dribble their ball was a small sacrifice to the determined and dedicated young basketball players. Night after night, Dad played on the street corner court. His shot became flawless and his passing ability was so refined that he compared himself to the great faker and passer of the Original Celtics, Nat Holman.

Dad's moves with the ball were catlike. The flurry of arms and legs, the scuffing of feet, the grunts and sweat seemed so natural to him. It was love at first shot.

In the beginning, the thought that his new idols, Joe Lapchick, Nat Holman, and Dutch Denhert were actually paid to play this game didn't even occur to Dad. He was infatuated with the pure sport of it. The competition fed his desire to excel and show off his athletic prowess.

After a year of street corner games, Dad was addicted to basketball. Despite the winter weather, his dedication never wavered. Every day was the same routine: go to school, run to the corner to play basketball. His violin lessons were history. He and his pals often played basketball well into the night, or until Officer Istock came by to enforce the city's curfew. At nine o'clock nearly every night, they'd see the huge figure of Istock coming down the road; and though they'd moan and groan, they would not argue with the affable, yet unrelenting officer. All the kids had a great deal of respect for Istock. He was not only the symbol of authority in Logstown, but he just happened to be a professional wrestler as well. Everybody knew Istock had tangled with the best, including the great Jim Londis, the world champ.

This routine went on for months, until one rainy day a dark figure in a suit walked up to their basketball court to observe the action. The boys noticed their spectator, but on their court a game only stopped for Officer Istock or a kid's parent. After a moment the man called out, "Boys! Who's the leader of this group?" They recognized the man as Reverend Anderson.

His voice was loud and authoritative enough to stop the action. Dad held the ball and looked around at his friends. A couple of the kids nodded at him, giving their support.

"That would be me, I guess." Dad cocked his head and stared curiously at Reverend Anderson.

"I'd like to talk to you, Press," he smiled. Reverend Anderson knew of my dad's love for basketball and thought it a good way to introduce him and the others to his Bible class. After a moment of contemplation, Dad flipped the ball to one of the boys and walked over to the reverend. A couple of words were exchanged, then the preacher and Dad started walking toward the Sunday school building not far from the corner. The boys at the basket were dying to know what was up. They watched as their leader disappeared into the building.

Inside, Reverend Anderson spoke candidly to Dad. "It's cold and rainy out there. You boys should have a place to play indoors. How about here?" The reverend's voice echoed through the large, barn-like building. He raised his arm and gestured as if he were giving the whole place to Dad.

Dad frowned and scanned the building. "Here? There are no baskets," he answered.

Reverend Anderson smiled, and said reassuringly, "We'll order them . . . real ones. We'll order everything." He watched Dad's face begin to radiate, then continued, "On one condition. I want you to come to Bible class three times a week . . . an hour each day."

Dad rubbed his chin and considered the proposal. He paced, feeling the weight of responsibility as a representative of his friends. It was cold outside, and he thought of how miserable it was playing in the rain and snow and how annoyed the gang became when they had to call off a game because of a downpour.

A few minutes later he ran back down the street to confer with his friends. By the time he got to them, he had his speech prepared. The kids gathered around, and Dad gave his first sermon about the benefits of Bible class. His speech included all the main ingredients, including real goals, real nets, and real basketballs. He also described how warm it was in that big barn and how even a blizzard couldn't make them miss a game.

"We can play in that joint, rain or shine!" he told them, knowing it as a key point, considering every kid on the corner was soaked to the skin. He reminded them that all they had to do was attend a few classes each week; a small price to pay to reap such enormous rewards.

"Well, what'll it be, men?" the reverend asked.

"We'll do it," Dad answered.

From that day on Bible class became a regular stop for the boys. Three days a week they studied Bible stories, and six days a week they played basketball indoors.

The change in my dad was remarkable. The controlled environment gave him the chance to work on his skills until he became a master of the fundamentals. The move indoors had its effect in other areas as well. Dad now talked about Abraham, Isaac, and Joseph the way he talked about Denhert, Lapchick, and Holman. Inspired by their newest heroes, the guys agreed on an official name for their team: the Daniel Boys. They admired Daniel's amazing courage in the lion's den, and they liked to compare his courage to theirs on the court.

For Dad a dream took shape in the form of a relatively new, untested sport called basketball. Thanks to Reverend Anderson and the Daniel Boys, he now could see a way to purchase his ticket and catch a train out of Logstown. Basketball would pay his fare.

3

Ten Bucks A Game

Playing basketball in a Sunday school building wasn't the big time for my dad, but it sure felt like it. His junior high years were the same basic regimen; up early in the morning and off to school; then evenings filled with playing basketball until Reverend Anderson sent him home.

Every night in the makeshift gym was like a professional game to Dad. He envisioned the roaring crowd as he pretended to play against the Original Celtics, or the New York Rens, or the Harlem Globetrotters. Every shot he made and every slick pass thrown were followed by waves of imaginary applause that filled the rafters of an imaginary coliseum.

Though the crowd response was confined to Dad's vivid imagination, the perfection of his skills became a noticeable reality, his quickness the most obvious attribute. Like lightning, he zipped past defenders. His hands quicker than most, his patented set shot was up and through the net before his opponents squared themselves to try to block it.

Dad's playing ability gained the respect of the kids who met him on the court and was recognized also by the older boys in town. The senior high school players in the Sunday school, the Brotherhood, knew a good young ballplayer when they saw one. After all they had experienced real competition, having played on the junior varsity and varsity teams. They forgot the age barrier and asked Dad to join them in some games. As a result he gained greater confidence playing against the larger, more aggressive players—guys like Steve Kaletz, Kramer, the Milanoviches, and Shorty Rebecca. It became obvious that my dad had the skill to become a quality ballplayer if he continued spending long hours in the Sunday school gymnasium playing against difficult opponents.

High school wasn't all fun and frivolous games to Dad; it was also a time to test whether all the hours of playing basketball in the Sunday school building would help him land a spot on the varsity. He was well aware that his high school basketball team traditionally consisted of five seniors due to the unwritten rule of no underclassmen on the squad, but he wasn't intimidated. He was an exceptional freshman; and his talents were quickly brought to the attention of the high school coach, Nate Lippe, by the seniors who had played on the Brotherhood team.

When he first saw my dad, Coach Lippe detected the attributes of a much older and much more experienced athlete. Having been a player for the Cleveland Brass, Nathan Lippe had seen his share of good ball handlers and shooters; and his keen basketball sense identified the Maravich boy as a diamond in the rough. With little hesitation, he put Dad on the team with five seasoned seniors, and Press Maravich became the talk of the campus.

Being on the high school team was a dream come true for Dad. He already admired his coach for a lot of reasons, mostly because Lippe achieved the goal that Dad so desperately wanted—to play professional basketball. Dad also admired a man who had the courage to break the unwritten rules and give an opportunity to a young kid who had the determination and desire to be his best.

Unfortunately, reality set in all too quickly. Even though my dad worked harder than ever, he found himself on the bench, a lonely sixth man on the team. The season started, and he wondered if he would ever see any playing time or merely remain an unwanted novelty in the league. Sure, he was a freshman on the varsity team, but it didn't matter much if he was "riding the pine," he thought.

Dad tried to rationalize why he wasn't getting to play. It couldn't be his shooting or ball handling, for he had proved his abilities over and over in practice. He wondered if Coach Lippe might be holding something against him, such as the day Lippe had called him off the court and asked him about the wad of chewing tobacco in his cheek. The coach had sternly told him to spit it out or expect no playing time. Dad remembered going down to the locker room that day and pretending to spit it out. Maybe he had been too much of a smart aleck when he came out of the locker room asking if Coach Lippe was happy now. Dad could have sworn he had fooled the coach just as he had Mrs. Banks. But maybe he hadn't.

The first part of the season was complete when the team arrived at Braddock High. Dad was thoroughly depressed when they got to the Pittsburgh school, realizing he would be sitting on the bench again. He figured it might not matter anyway since Braddock had crushed nearly everyone they faced the year before, and this year they were expected to do the same.

During warm-ups, Coach Lippe noticed his team was having difficulty getting good traction on the floor. He had them wipe off their shoes with towels dampened with car fuel they siphoned from their gas tanks. The old gasoline trick was a favorite of Lippe's; and on this night, he knew his team would need every advantage he could generate.

The game was closer than expected; and in the final minutes, with the game tied, my dad got the surprise of his young life. Coach Lippe pulled out one of the seniors and patted Dad on the shoulder. "Maravich," Lippe snapped. "Show me what you're made of!"

In a split second, my dad was up and into the game. Surprisingly, none of the first-game jitters accompanied him onto the floor. He felt as comfortable on this court as he ever had with the Daniel Boys at the Sunday school gym. With the clock running down, Dad scored two quick field goals to put his team on top. They never looked back. From that day on, Press Maravich rarely sat on the bench during a game.

The rest of Dad's high school days were filled with lots of hard work, both on and off the court. From that night in Pittsburgh, through the rest of his high school career, my dad became the leader of the team. Coach Lippe honored him as he named him captain of the team his junior and senior years.

Off the court, Dad landed a job in the mill as a pipe threader; and for three years, sleep became the lowest of all priorities. Dad learned responsibility firsthand as he worked, went to school, and played ball five days a week.

Through all the distractions, nothing seemed to diminish his intense love for Dr. Naismith's invention. He became an accomplished student of basketball, reading everything he could regarding the game. Unfortunately, few things were being written other than articles about the Original Celtics and other professional teams trying to make a go of it. Nevertheless, he continued analyzing the game he adored.

Only once did Dad attempt to head in another direction, and that was the summer he divided his evenings between basketball and baseball. It was almost un-American not to join the guys in sandlot baseball. But my dad thought if ever there was a sign from heaven as to which sport he should choose, it was revealed the day he met his match in the batter's box.

One evening he approached the plate with the authority of Babe Ruth. In his mind, the only difference between the Babe and him was the side of the plate on which they batted; Ruth was a lefty, Dad was a righty. Just like a pro, he dug in his left foot and waited for the pitch. He eyed the pitcher, and when a roundhouse curve came sailing at him, he dropped to his back to get out of the way. He jumped up, angry at the pitcher, until he heard the kid behind the plate yell, "Strike!" Dad realized then how cowardly he must have seemed dodging a simple curve ball.

He stepped back up to the plate, determined to stay in the batter's box regardless of the spin on the ball. That was his fatal mistake, because this time the curve ball didn't curve, but rather found its mark on the side of his skull. He was down and out, and spent the next few days in a hospital trying to clear the cobwebs from his head. When he finally managed to refocus his eyes, he could see clearly why he was going to stick with basketball, his first love.

Basketball was on the verge of exploding into a popular spectator sport in the United States in the 1930s. Despite the economic blow from the depression, teams still found a way to exhibit their talents and somehow make a living. The American Basketball League was intact, but the business of the game was still loosely structured and often a hit-or-miss proposition. The Original Celtics, perhaps the most successful professional team of the time, had the name and the clout to play a regular schedule and travel extensively. Other teams, such as the all-black professional teams, were limited in their ability to travel. The Harlem Globetrotters and the New York Rens were black teams confined to playing in the northern states;

but they still had an amazing effect on the game, helping spread the excitement of the sport all over the country.

The boom in basketball had a direct effect on my dad since professional scouts and coaches closely observed the high school ranks. Before long he was spotted by the Ambridge, Pennsylvania, team and was asked to join them in tournament play. Playing with this team was a great break for a high school player, and Dad jumped at the chance. Once again he found himself having to think up a new name since playing professionally disqualified him from high school competition.

He became known as Peter Munnell on the weekends and began traveling throughout the area under his assumed name. The money was nothing to brag about (ten bucks a game), but the experience and competition were invaluable. Tournaments began to spring up everywhere as basketball found its way into cities unfamiliar with the game, and at the same time Peter Munnell became a much-sought-after player.

His reputation followed him through Pennsylvania and Ohio. As a result, he started getting offers from other teams to join them on a tournament-to-tournament basis. In those early, loosely structured years, all a team needed was five good players who were willing to play at a moment's notice, and their squad could compete in a big tournament. Dad was called on nearly every weekend to join four other basketball-hungry young men. The trademark of the best of these "weekend warriors" wasn't the amount of money he had earned, but the number of gold basketballs that hung around his neck. Dad earned his share.

After several tournaments, the joy of winning a championship was instilled in Dad, and he could think of little else. His singleness of purpose and his unending dedication to basketball began to pay dividends even before he graduated from high school. He was actually earning money doing what he loved to do, and he gained a great deal of self-satisfaction knowing he had perfected his skills to the point of earning an income through the unique and exciting showcase of his talents.

Despite the lure of money, however, my dad was still well aware of the benefits of education. He knew too many people who were denied the chance to attend college, and he saw all around him the limitations that would be imposed on him if he didn't get a college degree. After he finished high school, he found himself in an unexpected position. Colleges were interested in him as a basketball player. Rather than having to resort to a college he could afford like most of his buddies, his hard work on the court opened doors to universities that offered him scholarships.

Because of his diligence in learning a strange new game, Dad now had choices about his future, and the dream of leaving Logstown was a reality. He was college-bound.

4

A Professional Collegiate

Duke University was the first to offer my dad a scholarship. But in the days before full-ride scholarships, partial scholarships were the only type available in athletics, and the Kosanovich family couldn't cover the difference.

With that in mind, Dad considered an offer from Long Island University. The great basketball pioneer, Clair Bee, coached the LIU Blackbirds, and my dad had heard stories of his brilliant coaching and inventive basketball mind.

The stories were true. Clair Bee was indeed a brilliant coach and quite prolific when it came to writing information on various aspects of the game. He wrote hundreds of books on basketball, books my dad studied throughout his career. It was said that if someone discussed with Clair Bee ideas regarding offenses and defenses or a philosophy of the game, before long, Coach Bee would write a book based on the subject of the discussion. Clair Bee ran a basketball camp in Red Hook, New York, where he perfected his theories with student athletes and professional players. He also traveled extensively with his clinics, spreading the good news of basketball philosophy to young and old alike.

One season, with a forty-one game winning streak on the line, Clair Bee's team faced the first ever seven-foot center, Clyde Lovellette of Kansas. In preparation for the game Coach Bee created the one-three-one zone defense. The defense proved effective and the giant seven-footer was stopped cold. Because of Coach Bee's creativeness, Dad considered LIU a front-runner.

Dad also pondered an offer to play for Coach Chick Davies at Duquesne University. But he considered Duquesne a little too close to home. For a kid who had always wanted to leave Pittsburgh, going to a Pittsburgh university would defeat his purpose.

Geneva College was added to the list, but as usual, his decision was ultimately influenced by ties to a friend. A best friend from Ambridge chose a small college in Elkins, West Virginia, and he asked Dad to join him. Dad didn't know much about the school, but he knew he would have a pal to help orient him to the new experience of college life and being away from home.

Davis and Elkins College has a picturesque campus nestled in the Appalachian Mountains, and when Dad arrived he settled quickly into his beautiful new surroundings. He decided to choose a normal, more stable career goal, so he applied himself to business courses. He became prolific in shorthand and typing, which came in handy for taking notes in class and preparing term papers.

Dad quickly made a name for himself and proved to be an extremely valuable asset to the college team. He played all four seasons at Davis and Elkins, and one year was among the top scorers in the nation. His grades were good and his athletic performance excellent, but he still faced the everyday challenge of trying to make ends meet.

The first two years were dreadful financially. Dad had a scholarship, but the school provided no money for room and board. The athletes were responsible for keeping a roof over their heads and food in their mouths. To make matters worse, the small town high in the mountains offered little as far as jobs were concerned.

Being ever resourceful, Dad overcame the problem by knocking on doors around town, securing jobs on his own. He offered his humble service each morning to families who desired the luxury of having their furnaces stoked in the frigid early morning hours. My dad knew how he hated waking up to a freezing house, and his instincts were right: people hired him immediately. Faithfully, before sunup, Dad entered eight unfamiliar homes and started their furnaces. At twenty-five cents a furnace, he accumulated a small but consistent amount of spending money.

Things remained pretty bleak until he reached his junior and senior years at D and E. "Peter Munnell" played professionally again, spending nearly every weekend traveling in a friend's car to Rochester, New York, where he was involved in tournament play against teams such as the Harlem Globetrotters, the Original Celtics, and the Rochester Royals. He earned one hundred dollars per game, and he unselfishly shared his earnings by feeding hungry athletes back in Elkins.

Dad was elected president of the student body his senior year, which demanded some of his time; but for the most part the rest of his college days meant basketball and more basketball. His only real diversion came when he signed up for naval flight training. He was eager to spread his wings and try something new, and that's exactly what he did. The United States Naval Reserve Air Corps offered free training through the college, and Dad saw it as an opportunity to do something wild and different. Unfortunately, he didn't comprehend the hasty decision he made when he agreed to instruction by the United States Navy. When he signed he also agreed to join that branch of the service if called upon.

Despite that small hitch, the training proved to be just what Dad needed. By the time he graduated from college, he had passed flight school with honors, winning the approval of his instructors and his family back home.

Now Dad had to officially go out into the real world. He was armed with a college degree, a pilot's license, and the skills to play professional basketball with any team that would have him.

To Dad's disappointment the only place he could find work was in his hometown, the place he had always wanted to leave. He spent the summer of 1941 in Aliquippa working as a pipe threader at Seamless Tube. It was depressing, but before long fall rolled around and he finally started doing what he did best—play basketball. His buddy Sam Milanovich and he landed a spot on the Clarksburg Pure Oilers team in West Virginia and began playing weekend games.

The third weekend of the season, the Pure Oilers met Dutch Denhert and the world champion Detroit Eagles. Dad had read about Dutch Denhert and the Original Celtics since he was a kid playing on the street corner. His adrenalin flowing, he put on an incredible show for his idol, ending the night with thirty points. After the game, Coach Denhert took Dad aside and offered him a contract to join the world champions for the rest of the season. Dad signed on the spot, fulfilling his dream of playing with the best in the world.

Being a member of a professional basketball team in the late 1930s and early 1940s was no easy task. The game was the easiest thing the players had to do. Staying healthy and getting to the auditoriums on time was the hard part. Basketball was a rough sport for tough men. People didn't pay to see the beauty of the new sport; they came to see action, lots of it. If that included bloody noses and cuts under the eyes from cheap blows, all the better.

Getting to the various cities was another challenge. The Eagles were one of several teams traveling the United States in large black touring cars. The schedule at times was incredibly tight, and all-night drives after a three-game day became normal.

Helping smooth the way for the Eagles was their team secretary, a clever young man by the name of Abe Saperstein, who created the fabulous Harlem Globetrotters. Saperstein traveled ahead of the Eagles, making sure all the schedules and accommodations were in order. He was also a master at generating interest in a team and getting them the best exposure possible.

He pulled one of his biggest publicity ploys the night the Eagles arrived in Chattanooga, Tennessee. The auditorium was sold out, and Saperstein eagerly anticipated a nice financial return at the gate. As the players warmed up before the game, the crowd applauded generously. But when the Eagles' coach, Dutch Denhert, walked onto the floor, the crowd noise was deafening. Dutch waved to the adoring crowd, and they cheered even louder.

The ovation had quite an effect on the team. They couldn't help but swell up with pride because their coach, now around fifty years old, was being received like a young superstar. To everyone's surprise, including Denhert and Saperstein, the crowd didn't let up but continued, louder and louder, calling for Dutch. Dad's heart raced with excitement; he wondered how an audience could be so mesmerized by one man. Then he remembered a story Coach Denhert had shared with the players on one of the long road trips.

About twenty years earlier, Dutch Denhert and the Original Celtics had arrived in Chattanooga and changed the look of basketball overnight. The Original Celtics were managed by an ingenious promoter by the name of Jim Furey, the man who first tried to make sense out of the business of basketball. In a day when teams were made up of different personnel every night, Furey developed the concept of signing five men to long-term contracts. Once the contract was signed they owed their allegiance to him. This proposition was attractive to the players who then enjoyed set salaries instead of unpredictable and haphazard percentage agreements made in each city.

On this particular night in the 1920s, five dead-tired ballplayers had stumbled off the train from Miami after a twenty-hour trip. Though they would never admit it, they could hardly function. Joe Lapchick, Pete Barry, Johnny Beckman, Benny Borgmann, and Dutch Denhert dragged themselves onto the court in Chattanooga wearing their wrinkled, filthy uniforms. The crowd was stunned to see the haggard, unshaven, lackluster squad. The team warmed up by taking a few unenthusiastic shots, then rested on the bench. At the same time, their opponents for the night, the Chattanooga Railites, were dressed in their sharp new uniforms. They were pumped up for the world champions, and their anticipation was obvious as they ran their new warm-up drills designed to thrill the ticket buyers.

But as usual, with the tip-off, the Original Celtics were impeccable. They were up by thirty points before the Railites knew what hit them. On this night, however, the quick scoring was due not only to the superior talent of the Celtics, but also to a maneuver Dutch Denhert happened upon quite by accident.

In those early days of basketball, some teams used a standing guard—a player who stood on his foul line throughout the game, even when his team had the ball at the other end of the court. Dutch volunteered to stand in front of the guy to keep him from breaking up the Celtic's fast break. What Dutch discovered was the ease by which he could take a pass from one of the fast-breaking players, then flip the ball in another direction or spin and take the ball to the basket himself. Dutch Denhert had invented the pivot play, and from that night on, his name was synonymous with the maneuver.

The Eagles and my dad were on that same court twenty years later and the Chattanooga fans had come to see the legend. Saperstein wasted no time as he saw what was unfolding. He convinced Dutch to go to the locker room and put on an Eagles uniform. After some hesitation, Dutch obliged Saperstein and the adoring fans by playing the game with his young team. My dad would never forget that night, the night he played on the same court with his childhood idol.

Dad grew close to his fellow Detroit Eagles during the seventy-five games he played with them. The long trips in the old touring car encouraged long conversations about politics, women, finance, religion, and basketball—but mostly basketball. They ate together, stayed up late drinking and playing poker, and shared every moment for weeks on end.

One Saturday the Eagles played three games: one at noon, one in the afternoon, and one that night. After packing the car for the all-night trip to New Orleans, no one volunteered to drive. Dad had a little energy left, so he crawled behind the wheel. He didn't let the fact that he didn't know how to drive get in his way. He drove down a lonely two-lane country highway, doing his best to keep the car between the ditches and keep his eyelids open. The night was exceptionally black with the moon totally concealed by clouds and no lampposts between towns to help him find his way. None of the players were awake. They were so beat they hadn't even discussed the games they had just played. Dad carried on, alone.

Suddenly, a cow wandered onto the road, and Dad hit the poor heifer. Though he was scared to death, he gained control of the car and pulled over to explain to the guys what had happened. Not one of them awoke. The next morning Dad tried to convince Coach Denhert and the team that the dent in the car had happened in a parking lot in the previous town. They had just overlooked it in their exhaustion. Somehow, they believed him.

Once the team arrived in New Orleans, Dad got some much-needed rest and prepared himself for the night's game. But before he could dress and get on the court, an unexpected telegram arrived at the front desk. The yellow slip of paper informed him that Uncle Sam wanted him to report in two days to Anacostia Naval Base in Washington, D.C. His last professional game before he fought for his country would be in New Orleans. He played his heart out that night and the next morning was on his way to earn his wings.

5

High Stakes

While traveling around the country with the Detroit Eagles my dad had sensed that basketball exhibitions were a welcome diversion to the American people whose minds were preoccupied with Hitler's aggressive war machine chewing its way through Europe. The war hit especially close to home for our family as the Nazis crushed Yugoslavia. Dad knew many of our relatives were held in subjection to the German regime.

When Dad received orders to report to Anacostia Naval Base in Washington, he figured that soon he would be in the rage of battle fighting for the freedom of the Maraviches and Kosanoviches in Europe. In December 1941, the Japanese shocked the world when they brought the war to Pearl Harbor. Dad listened to Franklin Roosevelt's famous speech denouncing the atrocity. The president warned his fellow citizens that the war had surrounded the United States and was closing in on the Western Hemisphere. Dad heeded his country's call to arms and considered it a privilege to do his part in preserving the way of life he so dearly loved.

Once Dad reported to Anacostia Naval Air Station for training as an aviator, it wasn't long before he was called into the commander's office concerning a matter of utmost importance. Dad entered the room like a seasoned military man and stood at attention waiting for the iron-jawed Navy man to bark out harsh orders. The commander turned in his swivel chair and sized up the lean new cadet.

"I see by your papers you were a professional basketball player. Is that true?" he asked.

Dad was caught off guard by the question. He frowned a bit, shrugged his shoulders, then answered, "Yes, sir, I am . . . uh, I was."

"Maravich," he grunted, "this base has a team that plays every alphabetical team in D.C."

"Alphabetical, sir?" my dad asked politely.

His commander smiled and with a nod said, "Alphabet. You know the IRS, the NRA, everybody has a team. I want you to coach my squad so we can smash a few bureaucrats. What do you say?"

A smile stretched across Dad's face as he considered the proposition. "It'd be my pleasure, sir," he answered.

This decision turned out to be one of the best Dad would make in his military career. While his cadet buddies were confined to the base eating mess hall food, he was constantly on the move with the team and dining on restaurant food.

Not only did Dad organize and run practices, but he would regularly leave the team during pregame warm-ups, order fifty or sixty burgers and colas to be picked up after the game, then distribute the booty to the cadets back on the base. He was assured a hero's welcome each time he returned from an outing. The cadets loved him for his thoughtfulness as well as for his taste in burger joints.

While Dad enjoyed the basketball aspects of his training, he was also becoming one of the hottest young pilots on the base. Like pumping in a fifteen-foot set shot, he adapted quickly to flying aircraft. His confidence in the air was comparable to his confidence and self-assurance on the court. His abilities won him the praise of the brass at the naval air station, but his proficiency and boldness also got him into trouble the day he buzzed a local prison in his Steerman aircraft.

Dad knew he was one of the best pilots on the base, and his brashness urged him to strut his stuff one afternoon as he soloed around the D.C. area. He figured it couldn't hurt if he displayed a few acrobatics for the inmates. He dove at the prison and tipped his wings to the cheering convicts.

A few minutes after landing and anchoring the biplane back at Anacostia, he was greeted unexpectedly by his commander. With a serious look in his eye he handed Dad a pick and shovel.

"What shall I do with these, sir?" Dad asked, dumbfounded.

"Cadet, there are big numbers on the side of that Steerman.

Surely it crossed your mind that the prison guards might report you," he answered. His face was stern and unchanging.

Dad swallowed hard. "Yes, sir," he replied in a guilty tone.

What followed was twelve hours of digging a hole six feet by six feet. Several blisters later, the lesson was learned. Dad never played games in an aircraft again.

After finishing training at Anacostia, Dad was sent back to New Orleans where he was placed in a "pool" with other pilots. All the pilots underwent more training, such as mastering Morse Code, as they waited for their next assignment.

My dad was told that the code was not only the primary means of naval communication but it could possibly save his life in a time of need. That was enough motivation to convince him to drill it into his head.

After New Orleans it was on to Pensacola where Lieutenant Maravich earned his wings as a Navy pilot. The instructors in Florida instantly identified his aptitude as a flyer. He had the brains and the physical dexterity that made a good pilot.

Earning his wings was not without pain, however. Dad's instructor, Colonel Smith, took him through his final qualifying test consisting of aerial acrobatics. He met the colonel out on the tarmac, eager to get the maneuvers over and the wings pinned to his uniform. Before they climbed aboard the aircraft, Colonel Smith gazed at Dad's cheek, trying to discover what he had stored in his mouth.

"What the heck is in your mouth, Maravich?" he asked bluntly.

"Chewing tobacco, sir," Dad answered nonchalantly.

"You're doing acrobatics with that junk in your mouth?" he questioned. My dad grinned and nodded. "Well . . . it's your funeral," Smith grunted as he shook his head in disbelief.

At ten thousand feet Colonel Smith took Dad through the qualifying moves. Dad was flawless in his execution. The plane acted as if it were a mere extension of him. He rolled and turned; he dove and climbed with the precision of a Swiss clock. After Dad completed the series, Smith shouted that he would like to take them through a power stall. The stall was the only move Dad hadn't done in the qualifying series. He took his hands off the stick and

41

raised them into the air, indicating to Smith that the machine was all his. Their bodies pressed against the back of the seat as the colonel raised the nose of the plane and put it in an immediate climb. He continued adding throttle, and the plane reached higher and higher into the blue sky until the engine could go no more. The engine stalled at the apex of the plane's ascent, and as expected, the plane flipped suddenly and headed straight down. What my dad didn't expect, however, was the sudden gulp of the majority of his chewing tobacco. Down his throat it went as the plane screamed for earth.

Colonel Smith knew all along what would happen. He listened as Dad's stomach emptied its contents into the cockpit. When the plane landed, an ambulance was waiting to take him to sickbay where he would spend an entire week trying to recover. Just the word *tobacco* sent him scurrying for a bed pan.

At the end of the week, Colonel Smith visited Dad in the hospital. Dad had to set aside his pride and ask him if it was thumbs up or thumbs down concerning his wings. Smith smiled and gave him a thumbs up. Dad let out a scream, startling every patient in the wing. But he didn't care—he had become a full-fledged naval aviator.

With wings pinned to his uniform, my dad left Florida for San Diego where he was to receive transitional training. When he reported to the commandant, a chief petty officer with stripes up to his armpits, surprised him with an unexpected question. "Where do you want to go, Alaska or the South Pacific?" he asked casually.

"Uh, there must be some mistake. I'm here for transitional training," Dad replied.

The CPO looked up from his clipboard. "The first one hundred pilots to come in here go to Alaska or the South Pacific, Maravich," he answered.

My dad was caught off guard. He turned to a friend he had made while standing in line. "What do you think? It's cold in Alaska and hot in the South Pacific," he asked.

"I dunno. Flip a coin," his friend replied.

Dad thought that sounded as logical as any other method. He flipped the coin, and by the time he reached the Hawaiian Islands the war with Japan was raging. The memory of the hundreds killed at Pearl Harbor instilled fierce courage in American pilots as they bombed the strings of Japanese-occupied islands throughout the South Pacific.

Before joining the fighting in Guadalcanal, Dad trained for a short time in Oahu, Hawaii. He was immediately given the job of coach for the base basketball team, and in a short time coached the team to the island championship.

Dad's best friend on the island was an all-American basketball player from Duquesne named Herbie Bonn. Dad enjoyed the company of another Pittsburgh pilot who loved the game of basketball. They shared hometown stories and struck up a great friendship.

The day they won the island championship, Dad and Herbie agreed to a big celebration feast. But first they had some night hops to get out of the way. The schedule read, "Napalm." At first they were confused because neither man had ever heard of Napalm Island. Later they found out Napalm wasn't an island, but rather described a new bomb the Navy was using.

As the sun began to set, Herbie and my dad had their planes on the runway ready for takeoff. Dad was instructing his copilot concerning night landings and takeoffs. As the engines roared, Herbie radioed over to Dad to remind him of the celebration. Herbie was expecting a great time in Oahu, so he thought he would warn my dad to be ready for a late night. Dad clicked his VHF and shouted back that he was ready for anything.

They laughed together as they taxied down the runway. Herbie looked to Dad and shouted, "After you, coach!"

Dad laughed and waved him off. "We couldn't have won it without you, Herbie," he gestured. "After you."

Herbie saluted and replied, "Fair enough." He positioned the plane for takeoff, then had a second thought. "Press, if this takes all night, we'll just celebrate all day tomorrow. Deal?" he shouted.

My dad saluted and said, "You bet."

Herbie's plane roared as the engines whipped the air. Dad felt good about himself and the great friend he had made through the common bond of basketball. As Herbie's plane cruised down the runway, he thought of how lots of guys from Pittsburgh must be making their families proud as they fought for their country.

At that moment Herbie's plane lifted off the end of the runway and suddenly exploded into an incredible fireball. My dad sat in his cockpit, numb. He couldn't believe his eyes.

The bomber was strewn across the airfield killing everyone aboard instantly. In the blink of an eye, Herbie was dead. At that moment my dad began considering the delicate barrier between life and death.

He parked his plane and despite his commander's orders, he refused to go up that night. He stayed drunk for three days mourning the loss of the best friend he had.

As the battle in the South Seas heightened, my dad joined a bomber squadron called the Black Cats, stationed in Guadalcanal. As a Black Cat he became the captain of the most important team of his life. He had a bombardier, a radio man, a radar technician, a mechanic, and gunners to handle the thirty-caliber machine guns. This team of brave men wasn't playing any games when they entered the fray of competition.

Bombing raids commenced at five in the evening and ended after five the next morning. With a basket of sandwiches and wing tanks full of fuel, Dad's crew was up in the air for the duration every night. The work was long and relentless as they spattered the tiny islands infested with the enemy. Hour after hour they dropped tons of bombs and dodged enemy antiaircraft artillery. When they ran out of bombs, they dropped empty beer bottles. The whistle a bottle issued on its way to the earth was enough to send the Japanese to their foxholes.

The nights were also spent on search and destroy missions aimed at Japanese shipping. Dad and his men looked for the blink of a light as the ships navigated their way through the war-torn shipping lanes. The sluggish cargo vessels were terribly easy targets for the bombers and soon carried the label of midnight coffins.

Dad and his Black Cat crew became quite proficient at their repetitious nocturnal flights. Flying through treacherous skys and over dangerous waters night-after-night tested their mental and physical capacities to the limit. They had great pride in themselves as they made a hit and received notice on the bulletin board at the base. Dad's crew had a long row of ships tacked to the board, and that recognition helped give their perilous task a silver lining.

One night they celebrated a direct hit on an enemy sub. It was dusk, but the bombardier was certain their load of bombs had sunk the unsuspecting vessel as it cruised the sea's surface. Dad and the men bragged of their success until the morning reconnaissance plane returned with some rather startling news. The commanding officer pinned a small replica of a whale on the bulletin board as the recon pilot described whale blubber strewn across the water.

When the men could find free time, they looked to athletics as a means of releasing the tension. As usual, Dad was given the enjoyable task of planning activities. The men pitched horseshoes, they played volleyball and softball, but most of all they enjoyed the basketball tournaments Dad organized. Despite the huge work boots the men wore, the competition was furious, and it provided a welcomed escape from the realities of war.

During his fifteen months of battle Dad encountered only one serious mishap. While on the ground at Canton Island, his squadron was surprised by a Japanese air raid. When the dust cleared, the Americans had suffered severe losses in ammunition and hardware, and Dad's VPB54 aircraft was one of the casualties. He was devastated, and his men thought it strange that he would shed tears over the loss of his aircraft; after all, no lives were lost. He eventually had to confess that he was shedding tears for the 350 packages of chewing tobacco he had stuffed into his parachute pack!

At the end of the fifteen months, Dad flew back to San Diego for R & R. The break was well deserved, since he had flown hundreds of missions with the Black Cats. Unfortunately, when he arrived at the base in California, he was immediately sent back into action.

Dad felt despondent and uncomfortable with a new crew and aircraft. He knew he would get to know his crew better than he knew his own family when all was said and done, but the disappointment of no time off left him depressed and uncaring.

As he flew, a storm on the horizon reflected the way Dad felt. He watched the rain falling in the distance and longed for those simple days when he played basketball on the street corner in the rain. As he got closer to the storm, he realized the intensity of it and wondered if his plane could handle the turbulence they were certain to encounter. Without hesitation he radioed for permission to return to the base. The request was immediately denied;

"Proceed to destination" was the message from the base. Dad analyzed his position. He couldn't go around the storm and he couldn't go above it. They were eight hundred miles from the base, so he was out of options. He ordered his radio man to repeat their earlier request. Again, permission was denied. Dad was hot.

His only option was to fly into the storm and hope. The thunderhead was awesome as the rain and wind began to hit the plane. Relying solely on his instruments, Dad lowered the aircraft to two hundred feet above the water, his altimeter the only thing keeping the seat of his pants out of the water. The young crew had no choice but to watch their captain carefully and trust him to see them through alive. All remained silent as the thunder clapped around them.

Visibility was zero for nearly two hundred nerve-wracking miles, then all of a sudden the bomber emerged from the darkness into brilliant sunshine. The guys broke into a cheer as Dad let out a whoop. He looked out his window to see the water shimmering underneath them. He could swear he could touch it, they were so low.

The whole crew breathed a sigh of relief as Dad climbed to a higher altitude. Feeling like a newborn baby, he laughed and shouted back to his navigator, "I need a new heading for Oahu. Get us home!" He waited for a reply, but didn't get one. Dad told his copilot to go back and find out what was going on. A minute later, the copilot came back and told him that his new navigator wasn't taking navigation. Dad was shocked, then he came unglued. He put the copilot in charge and made his way back to the navigator. In one swift move, he had his .45 caliber pistol out and under the navigator's chin.

Dad screamed, "What do you mean, you're not navigating! I oughta blow your head off!" The navigator admitted he had cheated on the navigation tests and didn't know how to navigate. The entire crew was stunned. Dad unloosed a list of American and Serbian curse words. The whole crew was on edge, wondering what my dad was going to do. The radar man pleaded with him to let the navigator go.

"This idiot has us lost over the Pacific Ocean! I gotta take care of you guys. We're running out of fuel." Dad barked.

After a pause, the radar man leaned in and replied, "Shoot him!" Dad put his gun back in his holster.

Dad had no time to deal with the guy. He slipped back into his captain's chair and stared death straight in the face. He didn't want to take the plane higher and waste fuel, so he maintained the low course. He and the copilot shared a worried look as they stared at an empty horizon.

My dad contemplated all the missions he had flown and all the antiaircraft fire that had zipped and pinged off the hull of his bomber. He had been spared so many times, but now to die plunging into the water from lack of fuel seemed so ridiculous, so stupid. He wondered if his dream of being a great basketball player had come to a senseless conclusion. And he wondered if all his ideas for the game would be left in his mind at the bottom of the sea.

After several minutes of maintaining the course and thinking of his premature death, Dad spotted a dot on the horizon. He rubbed his eyes, and as his plane got closer he saw an American ship coming toward him. He grabbed his lamp and signaled the ship, asking directions to the Hawaiian Islands. The ship's lamp blinked back, "Follow nose of ship." After another exchange, he figured the plane was off course about two hundred miles.

Before the guys stopped cheering about the new heading, Dad burst their bubble with news about the lack of fuel. He ordered his men to dump everything that wasn't needed. He considered dumping the navigator, but compassion overruled. They threw out their guns, ammunition—anything they could do without—to make it to land. They even threw the bombsight overboard, but not before Dad shot the lenses out of the eyepieces. He took no chances of giving any edge to the Japanese.

The plane was as light as possible as they crawled along the new path. Dad cut back so far on the lean mix that the plane shuddered and creaked. Like a crippled animal, the bomber made its way until they spotted the last island in the chain. Only Dad and the mechanic knew the fuel was down to near fumes. The crew gripped the closest solid object as they watched nervously and hoped for a safe landing. Dad radioed the tower for an emergency landing, and in a matter of minutes they spotted the airfield.

People emptied the hangars to watch the plane approaching the tarmac. A couple of emergency vehicles emerged from their garages and headed toward the runway.

Dad lined up the plane, and with the skill of a surgeon, brought the plane to earth. Once more the crew broke into a cheer until they realized the engines had just stopped cold: the fuel line was dry.

For the first time in his life, my dad felt he had experienced God's power in a very practical way. None of Preacher Anderson's best sermons ever affected him like an empty fuel tank and a raging thunderstorm. He would never forget the lesson.

6

Family Ties

Making it through his stint of World War II confirmed my dad's childhood belief that he was a survivor. He had stared death in the face countless times through bombing raids and escaped without a scratch. His dream of getting back on a professional basketball team and winning a world championship was still intact.

When he finally returned stateside, he knew he could do many things, but the thrill of the championship game at the Anacostia Naval Air Station, the Hawaiian Islands Championship, the tournaments in the South Pacific, and the championship games earlier with the Eagles lingered in his blood. He wanted nothing but basketball to challenge his competitive nature.

The war was winding down when Dad returned to serve as a flight instructor at Pensacola. Once the commander learned my dad was on the base, Dad was commissioned to coach the base's basketball team. Not long after that Paul Birch, the coach of the Youngstown Bears professional team, heard that Dad was nearing the end of his duty. Birch sent word to Florida that he wanted Dad to join his team in the National Basketball League. He had to choose between playing for the Bears or taking an offer from the government to teach the Chinese how to fly. The thought of flying over the Himalayas gave him enough reason to reject the offer. When he was discharged from the Navy, he exchanged his government issue uniform for a pair of shorts and a tank top sporting Youngstown's logo.

After thirty-one games as a Youngstown Bear, Dad got a call from Chick Davies in Pittsburgh. Chick was coaching the Pittsburgh Ironmen and he wondered if my dad still had a bit of the old spark he had seen before the war. My dad assured him that he did and was soon playing professional ball with the Ironmen.

By 1946 Dad was having the time of his life, and much of his dream was a tangible reality. He was earning decent money, and he traveled and played before appreciative fans. He didn't know exactly how great things truly were until one night after a particularly rough game when he dragged himself through his hotel lobby and a young lady seated at the taxi cab dispatcher's desk caught his eye. He couldn't help staring at her. She was lovely, with dark hair and dark eyes, and when she noticed Dad looking at her, she smiled a shy smile that captured him. He quickly forgot his fatigue and coolly sauntered over to her desk to turn on the charm.

"My name is Press Maravich," he said.

"Helen Gravor," she told him. "What's with all the stitches? You a boxer?" she asked, noting the sutures near his mouth and on his forehead.

Dad laughed, then explained to her the dangers of the most exciting sport in America—basketball. She was amused by his colorful explanation and his energetic way of bragging about his profession. They laughed a bit, and Dad sensed the chemistry already between them.

"Why don't you and I go out to dinner some night. What do you say?" He smiled and awaited her answer.

Helen pushed her hair behind her ear as she thought for a moment. "When?" she asked.

"Friday night? I'm off that night. Are you?" Dad questioned and hoped for the best.

"As a matter of fact, I am," she replied.

This news was the best he had gotten in weeks. She was beautiful, easy to talk to, and available. He couldn't ask for anything more.

Unfortunately, he unexpectedly headed out of town with the Ironmen and stayed out of town through Friday, missing the big date. He had been unable to reach Helen before leaving, and he knew she must be upset with him for standing her up.

When the Ironmen got back into town, Dad hurried to the dispatcher's desk hoping Helen would be there. She was. He took a deep breath and approached the desk. Before he could explain, he listened to her story of how she had gotten dressed and how she waited for hours for him to show. Dad pleaded stupidity and begged her forgiveness. Helen forgave him, and the date was rescheduled for Saturday night.

Saturday night came quickly. Dad had Helen on his arm as the two new friends entered Bill Green's Nightclub in Pittsburgh for an evening of dancing to the big band sounds. The band played great forties tunes, like "Chattanooga Choo Choo" and "I've Got a Girl in Kalamazoo," as they laughed and joked their way through the crowded club.

By the time they reached the dance floor for their first dance, they felt as though they had known each other forever. The music tempo slowed and Dad took Helen in his arms. She savored the moment in his strong embrace and stared into his eyes. Though the wounds on his mouth and forehead still held the seven stitches, his face seemed kind and sensitive, giving her a sense of comfort she had been missing for quite a while. His strong jaw and piercing eyes captivated her. Dad looked like a Hollywood star as he moved gracefully across the floor, leading his partner through smooth dance steps. They smiled constantly at each other as the music continued to create a romantic mood. She giggled as Dad took her into a slow, graceful dip, then brought her back up within inches of his face. She was without a doubt the most beautiful woman he had ever seen. Spontaneously, without warning, Dad blurted, "We should be married."

Helen was taken by surprise but didn't miss a step as the song accompanied their unusual conversation. "You're crazy. Married?" she asked, as if she were testing his sincerity, as well as his sanity.

"That's right," he replied with assurance.

She looked at him skeptically as the song faded and another began. A lot had happened during the first dance of their first date.

Helen soon realized that her date was quite serious with his proposal, even though it was seemingly an off-the-cuff remark. They continued to talk as the night progressed; and during the conversation, Dad learned more than he bargained for. Helen was very interested in a nuptial commitment, but with some strings attached.

Helen Montini was her married name. Her husband was one of

the unfortunate ones who had died trying to liberate Europe. Dad heard the story and had compassion for her. He assured her he knew there would be no way to replace her feelings for that man, but he could certainly be the husband she needed. This assurance was reassuring to her, but there was more. Helen had a three-year-old son, Ronnie, so any pact made with her was a package deal, and that had to be known and understood. Dad gave her his pledge to love her and her child, regardless of the circumstances. The next day they got blood tests.

What followed was an enormous wedding including Dad's six best men. The reception bill was tallied at seven thousand dollars, an enormous sum in 1946. Over seven hundred well-wishers, including Navy buddies and basketball friends, crowded the reception hall to celebrate the marriage of Press and Helen Maravich.

After the bill was paid by donations from the guests, Dad and his new bride headed for Chicago for a romantic honeymoon. Since the romance had been so sudden, the honeymoon became the place to start getting to know each other. They shared stories of their childhoods and memories of their families and friends. After hours of reminiscing, the heart-to-heart discussion took an unsuspected turn. Dad told her that he was a bomber pilot in the war, then informed her of his interest in becoming an airline pilot. Because of the good income and prestige of the job, Dad assumed she would be excited and impressed with his sense of responsibility. But her reaction caught him off guard. Instead of approving of his respectable, well-paying job, Helen harshly disapproved of it. She didn't care that the position would bring financial stability to her home; she imagined the instability it would bring to her peace of mind. She didn't want her husband in airplanes. They were too dangerous, and she wouldn't stand for it. She let it be known he would have to choose between her and his airline job.

The ultimatum leveled, Helen sat back and waited for Dad's answer. He loved her and cherished their new relationship. He saw the concern in her eyes, remembering how she had so recently lost her first husband, the father of her child.

"Okay. What do you suggest I do to support us?" he asked, quietly.

"Every story you've told me concerns coaching basketball. How about that? What about basketball?" she asked with a hint of pleading in her voice. She knew how much he adored the game, and she figured the suggestion was practical and would end the debate between them. She was right.

"For you I'll go into coaching," he replied.

Because of the love Dad had for Helen and the fear she had of losing him, he made the choice that would pattern their lives—and mine.

BOOK TWO

THE HEIR APPARENT

7

Born To Play

Dad moved his family of three back to Aliquippa, Pennsylvania, where he taught at his alma mater and coached basketball. Ronnie was active and strong, and life was good to them. Best of all, Mom didn't have to worry about her husband crashing an airplane. He was rooted solidly to the Aliquippa gymnasium floor.

On June 22, 1947, Dad found himself in the waiting room of a hospital, eager for the arrival of the newest addition to the family. Mom was in the first stages of labor as the doctor passed Dad in the waiting area.

"Doc, make a little wager with me, would you?" he asked as he caught the doctor by the arm.

"Now, Press, you know I'm not a betting man," the doctor smiled. They had been carrying on in this manner for quite a while, and the doctor knew how much my dad was yearning for a baby boy. "I guarantee it's one or the other," he laughed.

"Well, I'm telling you now, if it's a girl, you pay the hospital bill. If it's a boy, I pay," Dad chuckled as he wiped his sweaty palms. The doctor reluctantly agreed. By this point, he would promise anything to get my nervous father to relax and leave him alone.

A few hours passed, and the doctor emerged with a grin on his face. Dad looked him in the eye, waiting for the verdict. The doctor toyed with him for a moment.

"Well . . . ," the doctor wiped his brow, "you pay, Coach."

Dad let out a holler that could be heard in every wing of the hospital. The plans he had for me made him shake with anticipation. "We're calling this boy Peter Press Maravich, Doc! Remember that name," he said, shaking the poor doctor's hand too hard.

"How's Helen?" he asked, realizing his excitement had excluded her.

"She's fine . . . and your boy's fine," the doctor replied.

When Dad first laid eyes on me, he swore then and there that I had the potential to be a great basketball player. "Look at those hands! Look at his feet! The kid's got it, I tell you," he said, as he grabbed nearby hospital personnel. The doctors and nurses failed to see the signs, but to Dad I had basketball written all over me.

He wanted so much to nurture me and direct me so that I might be able to attain even greater things in my life than he had. As a coach, Dad knew he would be able to provide the necessary instruction and environment for me, considering the hours he normally spent in a gymnasium. But implementing his plan would happen later. After all, I had to grow a bit before he could start teaching me anything related to basketball.

Coaching basketball consumed Dad's every thought. But coaching high school basketball offered little income, and when money got tight he was forced to make some decisions. He had four mouths to feed, and the salary at Aliquippa was inadequate to sustain them.

Coach Red Brown called from Davis and Elkins, asking Dad to join him as an assistant coach. This offer was just what Dad needed. The position would get him into the college ranks, and he would be coaching in familiar territory with a good friend.

He accepted the position, which offered a little more pay, and began recruiting Pennsylvania boys to fill the roster of the West Virginia school. His instincts were correct. The starting five he found in the Pittsburgh area continued playing together for four years and racked up an impressive seventy-eight wins and fourteen losses. Dad was a winner; and success on the court wasn't just fun, it was a requirement.

While enjoying the success at work, my dad continued to watch his sons grow. Every evening after Mom's delicious dinners, Dad went into the backyard and shot baskets, knowing all the while I was observing every movement. I was so impressed as I watched him pump in shot after shot without missing. His plan worked very well. He knew almost any son would want to copy his father, and if his calculations were correct, I would be drawn into the sport he worshiped.

In 1947 and 1948, my dad accepted assistant coaching jobs at Davis and Elkins, and then at the University of West Virginia. He took Ronnie and (later) me to all the games and practices. As soon as I was old enough, though the ball was half my size, I began dribbling constantly in the gym, acquiring a skill for bouncing the ball on a wooden surface.

As Dad helped me work on my skills, he continued pushing himself intellectually. At West Virginia, he finished his requirements for his master's degree in health education, writing a thesis outlining scouting for basketball teams. He had done plenty of it and saw the need for a comprehensive handbook for basketball scouting. With financial backing, he put the book into print, making it the first of its kind in the marketplace.

Dad's attention to detail and his fervent study of the game captured the interest of many schools looking for good, intelligent coaching. In 1949, he landed his first head coaching job. West Virginia Wesleyan offered him thirty-five hundred dollars a year to coach, and he couldn't afford to let pass that jump in pay.

As a head coach on the university level, Dad felt he had achieved another important personal goal. He called all the shots for his teams and answered to no one but himself when it came to scouting, recruiting, designing plays, and motivating the players. He was on his own, and it was time to experiment with the game he knew inside and out.

Dad thought of writing another book: An in-depth look at the psychology of basketball. He had some theories he needed to test before writing about them; and since he was head researcher with a court full of guinea pigs, he seized the opportunity.

Dad secured the services of a Czechoslovakian psychiatrist who had come to America to escape the Nazi invasion of her country. He designed thirty questions for Dr. Seary to ask his players. They were simple questions regarding their families, their school, their coach, and so on. During a one-on-one session with the doctor, the boys wrote their responses on a sheet of paper and turned them in for evaluation. After the tests, Dr. Seary analyzed each player and gave her results to Dad. She discussed her findings and related to him different aspects of the students' backgrounds and how best to instruct them in order to achieve optimum responses on the court.

Dad took all the results and mulled over them. After hard study, he hit upon his technique for coaching his newest squad of basketball players. He created his own psychological approach for his team and implemented it throughout the entire season.

When the season began, the team quickly developed into a highly motivated, highly skilled unit. But the players noticed something strange about their coach. It seemed that Coach Maravich always screamed at George, the starting forward. George was no wizard of the game, but he didn't seem to deserve the horrible tongue lashings Dad dished out constantly. If he wasn't yelling at George, he was yelling about George and the stupid mistakes he made. The rest of the team listened intently, knowing they were just as guilty as George most of the time, but Dad never reprimanded them; just poor George. Sometimes he sent the rest of the team out after half time, and kept George in the locker room for more discussion. The Wesleyan players didn't know what Dad said when they were gone, but it didn't matter. They were just happy to be out of his line of fire.

The season ended with Wesleyan being beaten in the championship game by Davis and Elkins—the five boys Dad had recruited for his alma mater. Dad had steered the team to twenty wins and six defeats. After the last game, he congratulated his team, and praised them for their hard work and cooperation. During his talk, one of the team members mustered the courage to ask Dad why he was always so hard on George.

Dad laughed and assured the team he thought George was one of the best players Wesleyan had. In fact, he liked George a lot. Then he leveled with the team, telling them Dr. Seary's conclusions. George had a hearing impairment that excluded loud volume. When Dad screamed at the kids, blaming George for everything, George hadn't heard a word. When the players left him alone with George, he spoke softly and praised George for his play. His apparent disapproval with George seemed to motivate the entire team, so he stuck with it the whole season!

The Wesleyan players were totally impressed with their coach, calling him a "genius" and a "great psychologist." Dad just nodded at them and smiled, knowing he had the material for the first chapter of his book.

At the end of the year, Red Brown left Davis and Elkins to take the head coaching job at the University of West Virginia. Without hesitation, Red and most of the board of trustees came after my dad to be assistant coach. The newspapers touted the duo as the two best coaches around, saying the university was ready for great years of basketball. Dad took the position and began recruiting players, but before the season began, another college came knocking at his door. Davis and Elkins wanted him to come back to take the place Red Brown had vacated. They came with money, luring him with a higher salary of five thousand dollars a year, plus a two thousand dollar bonus just for taking the job.

This offer was more money than Dad had ever seen as a coach, and the deal looked very attractive. Dad had a long talk with Red, but despite Red's warning, he left the UWV job and returned to his alma mater to be head basketball coach. To Dad, it was a matter of economics; he had a family to feed and clothe, and the bill collectors were hounding him. Red warned Dad he would never see the money, but in an act of faith, Dad packed up and hoped for the best.

In 1950, we arrived back in Elkins and Dad began his coaching duties. To his surprise, however, much more would be required of him than merely coaching a team. He was also asked to serve as athletic director, teach shorthand and typing, and act as assistant coach for the football team. He took it all in stride. After all, he would be making seven thousand dollars in one year, and he was certain the money would take care of his obligations.

Unfortunately, the words of caution from his good friend, Red Brown, came back to haunt Dad. Not only was he denied the two thousand dollar bonus, he also had to sue the president every month to get his pay check!

Dad tried desperately to work through the difficult circumstances, but it became too much to bear. We needed money. He packed up the family once again, and in the fall of 1952, accepted a position at Baldwin High School in Pittsburgh.

Baldwin High was a tough inner-city school. It was the classic "blackboard jungle," complete with gangs, hoods, and switch-blades. Dad hated the rebellion he saw, so he decided to try to make some changes.

He asked the principal to call an assembly of the entire student body. He saw the phenomenon of long hair making its way into the school, and he knew it was predominantly worn by roughnecks. The particular style he was out to change was characterized by a small flip at the neckline called a ducktail. Dad's plan involved an all-out assault on the ducktail and the dead-end world of apathy and troublemaking it represented.

Seven hundred fifty students listened as my dad presented his idea for a club called the Crewcut Club. The club would have parties and athletic activities for everyone. The school facilities were at their disposal for recreation, and the kids would collectively make up the rules and bylaws of the club. The idea posed some exciting possibilities for independent-thinking students.

At the end of his speech, Dad encouraged all interested students to stay and help plan the club; the rest were excused. The principal released the students and Dad sat back waiting for throngs of kids to respond. Five minutes later he was standing alone with four students.

Never one to admit failure, Dad continued with the club. Before the year was out, he had several hundred members attending meetings and activities. Delinquency in the school dropped dramatically.

Dad's most rewarding experience at Baldwin happened after the first week of teaching. The principal knocked on the door of Dad's classroom wanting to speak with him. He went to the door, wondering why he was being disturbed in the middle of class.

"I have something for you," the principal said, as he took an envelope from his suit pocket.

"What's this? I'm fired already?" Dad joked.

"It's your check," the principal said.

Dad was stunned. He took the envelope and opened it to see a check for his first week's wages. He was so overcome, he had to step into the hall to wipe the tears from his eyes. The principal was aware of the troubles Dad had suffered in his last job. "You don't have to sue me, Press," the principal quipped.

My dad shook his boss's hand and went back into the class a happy man. That night, Mom and Dad pinned the check to the kitchen wall and stared at it as they ate supper. They realized how the little things in life can be taken for granted.

At home Dad still shot baskets in the backyard every night. At five years old, I imitated my father as much as possible. Still, despite my pleading to take one shot, Dad denied me, saying I was too little. He told me I would have a chance when I grew up, if I was still interested. I squirmed with anticipation as his baiting process continued. Building this anticipation was all part of his dream for me.

A year later Dad got a call from an old friend, one of his buddies from the Daniel Boys in Logstown. His friend had become the principal at Aliquippa High School, and he wanted Dad to come home and coach basketball and teach physical education. Once again, my parents sat down with the family budget and worked out the numbers. Aliquippa was offering sixty-five hundred dollars a year for teaching and coaching duties. That salary combined with a summer job at the old steel mill would keep us in good shape and hold off some bill collectors. Dad took the position.

The day Dad arrived, he noticed the school had hung a picture of him on the wall—a picture of him in his white Navy uniform, a symbol of courage and American pride. He felt honored knowing someone respected what he had done.

Dad felt at home right away as he got started in the new job. He took inventory of his sports equipment and organized the department, preparing himself and the facilities for the new year. Even the gym floor received a new finish.

The first day of class Dad felt proud as he walked out onto the new floor in his basketball shoes. The students seated in the bleachers gave the new coach a good looking over. They had heard all about the ex-professional basketball player, and they had also heard of his exploits in World War II. They watched as my dad opened his roll book and read off the names in an authoritative, yet gentle tone.

With everyone present, Dad informed them of a few rules everyone would adhere to if they wanted to remain in his gym class. The students gave a few grumbles, but he paid no attention. He opened his book again and began reading, "Rule number one: No one walks on this gymnasium floor without basketball shoes on their feet." Dad's voice echoed through the large room. He took a breath to read the second rule, but before he could speak a student mumbled, "Big shot Navy man."

Dad didn't look up. He was surprised, but didn't let anyone detect his reaction. He slowly raised his book in order to peer over it and watch the students. He continued, "Rule number two: Every person who participates in any physical activity will be required to take a shower afterward."

Again, a voice from among the students was heard saying, "Big shot Navy man."

Dad tried to maintain his cool, but he could feel the blood coming from his feet all the way up to his face. Though the pressure was building, he continued the rules. "Rule number three: If you're late for class, you don't dress out," he said as the blood pumped harder.

"Big shot Navy man," the student echoed.

That was all Dad could take. He threw the book across the floor and charged into the stands. The innocent students parted like the Red Sea, leaving the guilty kid alone for the kill. In one swift move Dad had the kid by the collar throwing him down the bleachers onto the floor. He grabbed his paddle nearby and began paddling the rebellious youth while spitting out every curse word he knew. Between the cursing, Dad threw in some appropriate comments like, "ungrateful," "hood," "disrespectful," and "spoiled," as well as several Serbian words only a few kids could comprehend.

Dad was beside himself with anger. He couldn't believe the lack of discipline he had encountered in the first few minutes of school. After the final swat, he turned to the rest of the students, asking who was next. The class sat terrified. When he saw no takers, Dad headed toward his offfice, passing the school superintendent who had watched the whole ordeal from a distance.

"What on earth is happening, Coach?" he asked.

This wasn't a good time to approach Dad. He grabbed the super-intendent and screamed, "What kind of school are you running here! These kids have no discipline at all!" Dad left the superintendent shaking and stormed into his office. He slammed the door, and all was silent.

A few minutes later the principal knocked on Dad's door. "Press! Press, what the heck is going on? Are you all right?" he yelled through the door.

"Leave me alone," Dad answered.

The principal couldn't leave him alone. He had known my dad too long, and he knew things could be worked out. After several minutes of encouragement, Dad finally calmed a little and opened the door. The principal and Dad had a long talk, which finally reassured Dad and convinced him to return to the class. Little did he know that that one action established him as the school's chief disciplinarian. By the end of the year, he had several paddles on the wall with the name of each victim written on them. They hung like trophies, representing Dad's firm belief in discipline.

In the first week of school, Dad confiscated over three hundred knives from students' lockers in a sweeping display of authority. The school was still rough, regardless of his presence, but it was a little safer to walk the halls knowing Coach Maravich roamed them with his trademark Louisville Slugger.

One evening after a rough day of teaching and muscle flexing, Dad walked out to the backyard basketball goal to shoot baskets and clear his mind of the challenges at Aliquippa High. It had become a familiar sight for him to see me watching in the distance, and this day was no exception. For a couple of years, the ritual of evening shooting had been going on, and Dad was beginning to wonder how well his plan was working on me. Mom and Dad's plan was to make me basketball hungry. They felt if I had the liberty to play basketball as I did all other games, my commitment would not be as strong. They had been trying to drive home the point that basketball was much more serious than all my other pleasurable activities.

At Christmas time they bought me my very own basketball, but I had become distracted by an old trumpet. Dad wondered if he should abandon his scheme to draw me into the game and use a more direct approach. He called to me as I peeked around the corner of the house, just as I had done so many times before.

"Pete, where's your basketball?" he asked.

"Inside," I answered casually.

"Come over here and take a shot," Dad said.

Dad was ready to instruct me on how to shoot a basketball. He placed my hands correctly on the ball, and I bent down ready to shoot a set shot. I pushed the ball high in the air toward the goal and missed completely. Dad's eyes quickly went to me to see my reaction. It was just what he had hoped. I was angry that I had failed, consequently I ran to the ball and angrily shot it again, again, and again. When Dad saw I was attracted to the game, he knew his plan had succeeded. I was hooked for good.

I was so slightly built, Dad had to smile as he watched me shoot. I took the ball down to my bent knees, then lunged my whole frail frame at the goal. My form may have looked elementary and strange, but Dad didn't care how it looked; he merely cared that he had nurtured in me an interest in the game.

When Mom called us in for dinner, Dad and I had a tough time stopping. It was great being with my father—my hero. Dad enjoyed spending time with me as well. We took a few more shots, then stopped to have a heart-to-heart talk.

"Basketball's fun, isn't it Pete?" he asked with a serious look on his face.

"Yes sir, it is," I answered politely.

He knelt down and looked me in the face. What he was about to say was the key to his plan, and it was important that I hear every word and read the sincerity in his eyes.

"You've seen me do my summer camps, and teach kids how to play basketball, right?" he asked. I nodded. "I'm teaching kids to play a game that can open a whole future for them. For some, basketball is their key to going to college. I want you to know, your mother and I can't afford to send you to college. But with my teaching and many hours of practice, you could possibly earn a scholarship that would pay for your education. And you know what? If you become really good, you might even play pro basketball like I did, and they'll pay you for doing it!" My eyes lit up. "And then you may play in the world championship game," he continued, "and if you win that game, they'll give you a big diamond

Press Maravich, Naval aviator.

Dad and Mom, Aliquippa, PA., 1947.

The family in 1957.

Peeking over Dad's shoulder (that's me on the far left) I learned much about basketball strategy.

High School huddle (No. 23 is my hero, brother Ronnie; I'm No. 3 facing the camera).

"The Pistol" taking aim (8th grade).

Diana and Dad.

High School ball in North
Carolina.

Dad and I arrive at LSU.

Another launch at LSU.

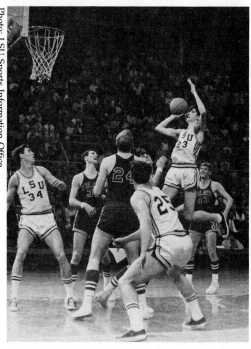

Photo: LSU Sports Information Office

Photo: LSU Sports Information Office

Is "The Pistol" out
of ammunition?

Passing the ball through my
opponent's legs.

Playing "Celtics ball."

I've always loved helping kids learn how to play basketball.

Becoming a member of the National Basketball Hall of Fame, May 1987. From left are Rick Barry, Walt Frazier, Bob Houbregs, myself, and Bob Wanzer.

AP/Wide World Photos

ring . . . and on that day, they'll say Peter Press Maravich is one of the twelve best players in the world."

The words rang in my head like nothing I had ever heard. I stood alone watching my father walk toward the house, thinking over and over of the diamond ring and being one of the best in the world. Dad knew the seeds were sown and taking root.

Dad saw my determination as I started spending every evening with him learning basketball. The dream officially had passed to a new generation.

8

Pass The Ball

In the fall of 1955, Dad applied for the head coaching job at Clemson University in Clemson, South Carolina. He was so eager to return to the college ranks, he paid little attention to the salary being offered. He was bringing home so little at the secondary level that he assumed the pay at a major college would dwarf his current income.

Frank Howard was the Clemson athletic director and head football coach at the time. He called one of his recruiters and close friends, Neenie Campbell, to see if he had heard of a basketball coach by the name of "Mahvich." Neenie said he knew of Maravich, and recommended he be hired immediately. He went on to say he was a good Yankee. Howard said, "There ain't no good Yankees!"

Regardless, he set a date to meet Dad in June. Dad drove from Aliquippa to Clemson and introduced himself to Frank Howard, Banks McFadden, General Bob Jones, Bob Smith, and Bob Bradley. When Dad walked into the room, Howard said, "Have you guys ever seen a dang Yankee before?"

Howard took Dad into a room and showed him a list of over a hundred applicants for the coaching job and he growled, "Why should I hire you, Yank?"

Dad was sure of himself and retorted, "I can coach better than any of those guys. Give me a chance." With no commitment in hand, he turned around and drove all the way back to Aliquippa.

Two months later, Neenie Campbell called to tell Dad he had the job. Dad was shocked to discover he would have to take a two thousand dollar pay cut for the chance to coach on the major college level, but he felt it was worth it.

With high hopes we arrived in Clemson, South Carolina, and Dad began his head coaching duties. He soon found himself trying to rationalize the job change to my mother. She was stunned to find he was being paid a slim ninety-six dollars a week to create a basketball program.

Ever the optimist, Dad planted the necessary seeds to get the new program off the ground. Once again he had to generate interest in basketball when football was the predominant attraction. He swallowed his pride and tackled the challenge.

Coach Howard strongly urged Dad to recruit basketball players from South Carolina as a show of state pride and also to please the board of trustees. But Dad still harbored a prejudice for Pennsylvania players. He felt he knew the kind of coaching they had been receiving for years and still considered the state second only to New York in producing raw talent. His strong will prevailed, and the freshman team consisted of five Pennsylvania youngsters.

Unfortunately, the team didn't fare well and took a beating their first season. Knowing Coach Howard was breathing down his neck, Dad drilled his chosen ones into a tightly knit unit and started winning some ball games the second year.

As Dad's Clemson Tigers improved, he simultaneously became one of the most popular coaches on the East Coast with his colorful coaching antics and his humor. The opposing coaches quickly became friendly rivals, visiting him at Clemson or at our home for a discussion of basketball philosophy and strategy. My Mom always brewed fresh hot coffee for Dad and his coaching buddies in anticipation of the late nights of basketball rhetoric. He had a wealth of knowledge to draw on, and like a wise old sage he was willing to talk with anyone who wanted to knock around new ideas or reminisce about old ones. Late night discussions were especially formative times for me. When I heard Dad haggling with his coaching friends, I used to sneak downstairs and sit on the edge of the stairway listening to basketball strategy into the wee hours of the morning.

One of Dad's best coaching buddies was Bones McKinney of Wake Forest. McKinney had quite a reputation himself when it came to bringing excitement to basketball in the ACC (Atlantic Coast Conference), and Dad could relate to a true lover of the game.

They spent hours arguing about what college basketball should and should not be. Sometimes they agreed, and sometimes they loudly disagreed. But regardless, they enjoyed each other's approach to the game and shared some good competitive moments on opposite sides of the court.

One season Dad's team met Bones and his squad for the annual conference game. To Dad's surprise he saw McKinney across the floor standing with the Reverend Billy Graham. Bones smiled, made the sign of the cross, and gave Dad the thumbs down.

After McKinney and Rev. Graham disappeared into the locker room, my dad sneaked to the other side of the gym and walked in on the great evangelist speaking to the Wake Forest team. It only took a moment for Dad to get Rev. Graham's attention and demand equal access.

"I have boys on my side I'm trying to save, too, Reverend," he started. "How about a little word to the good Lord about my Tigers?"

Bones couldn't believe the gall of his friend, bursting in and demanding equal time from his inspirational ace-in-the-hole. Dad just smiled at McKinney as Rev. Graham left to speak with the Clemson team. The Tigers won the game!

As Dad changed the face of Clemson basketball, noticeable changes were ocurring in the Maravich family. Dad seemed to spend every waking moment at Clemson. If he wasn't in the middle of a basketball season, he was preparing for the next, recruiting players and creating basketball strategies. Ronnie was growing more and more independent, especially since entering high school. He was a gifted athlete with the renegade spirit of James Dean's rebel, and Ronnie never found a reason to spend time at home.

Because of my dad's constant absence from home, Mom became even more the backbone of the family. She approached her duties as homemaker and mother with the tenaciousness one would expect from her head coach husband. The money was difficult to stretch, but even in the lean times, she made certain Ronnie and I never went hungry or entered public in worn clothes. She had great pride in her family and was determined to hold down the fort even when elements of growth and change were trying to pull us apart.

Mom had tremendous insight into my development as an athlete. One evening she watched out the kitchen window as Dad and I played one-on-one. The will to win was so ingrained in my dad that he wouldn't allow me to come close to winning. He wanted his son to rise to the challenge and learn there are no free rides to success. After another loss, I walked into the house and disappeared gloomily into my room. Dad entered the house a short time later, shaking his head, disappointed in me. "I don't know what's with that kid. He seems so uninterested in basketball. Sure, he shoots the ball and fools around a lot, but he's got no guts," he said as he took his seat at the table.

Mom pulled up a chair and quietly said, "Why don't you let him win . . . just once."

Mom's words hit Dad like a brick. Not until then did he realize how foolish he was being with me. He was trying to get his son hooked on a game he loved, but he didn't have the sense to ease up on the competition and let me get a taste of winning. He just sat for a moment, thinking about what he had done, then he took Mom's hand and said, "You married a big dummy, Helen." Mom shook her head and smiled, assuring him she thought quite the opposite.

Dad came to my room and found me lying on my bed, very depressed. "Pete, one more game before you go to bed? Come on, it'll do you good," he said.

I didn't feel like being beaten again, but I respected my dad and obeyed his request. After a quick game of Twenty-one, Mom heard the back door burst open and me shouting through the house, "Mom, Mom, I beat Daddy! I beat Daddy!"

Mom met me in the hallway with a congratulatory hug. Dad was at the back door as he listened to my excited explanation of the game.

That night was a turning point for all of us. The foundation was laid, and it was then Dad saw my need for serious instruction. He wanted desperately for me to master the fundamentals of basketball, but at the same time keep the fun in it.

Dad devised a method of teaching me that would later become

known as "Homework Basketball." The first lessons he taught were in the area of shooting, since that was the most fun and the most complicated.

Dad introduced me to the concept of image shooting, or conceptualization. He told me to imagine a little man who played basketball all the time. When I shot the ball, the little man shot the ball. The only difference was that the little man never missed. After hours of shooting, I developed an instant picture of the little man shooting and the ball going through the hoop. Eventually, before every shot I attempted I pictured the ball through the hoop before it left my hand. Dad designed the technique to give me confidence before every shot.

My dad analyzed my shooting form as I progressed. During one workout he noticed I was missing a lot of shots and getting discouraged. He instructed me to shoot short lay-ups until I made 50 percent and got my confidence back. If I attempted ten shots, and only four went in, I was under 50 percent—an unacceptable percentage. I would then move in closer to the basket and shoot lay-ups until I raised my average over the 50 percent mark. This gimmick helped my concentration as well as my confidence.

Another ploy to keep my interest was encouraging trick shots. The basic jumper became monotonous for me, so my dad showed me every trick shot he knew including behind the back, between the legs, bouncing it in off the ground, and so on.

This intensity of learning and experimenting never stopped. I began to eat and sleep with my basketball by my side. I was so dedicated to perfecting my skills that when Mom came in to kiss me good night, without fail I was lying in bed shooting the ball to the ceiling and catching it. I'm sure she heard me repeating, "Finger tip control, backspin, follow-through . . . finger tip control, backspin, follow-through."

As Mom said good night, she would tuck the ball under my arm, as some mothers would a child's Teddy bear, then turn out the light. Sleep didn't come easily because my mind constantly churned new ideas regarding the ball-handling and dribbling drills my dad had taught me that day.

Without fail, the next day I was up and at it once again. By age thirteen, the basketball had become an extension of me and my personality. I knew its dimensions as well as I knew the back of my hand. I had become a basketball android.

The citizens of Clemson soon grew accustomed to seeing me with a basketball in my hands at all times. I even dribbled as I walked the two miles to town. I dribbled nonstop, alternating hands to make certain I would be as skilled with my left as with my right. After several months of the routine, the two miles suddenly became much easier when Mom and Dad scraped up the money to purchase a bicycle. Then I raised a few eyebrows dribbling with either hand while riding the bike to town.

Handling the ball became another obsession for me, and I convinced myself I could dribble under any condition. After carefully blindfolding myself, I dribbled my ball through the house, learning the placement of the furniture and the sounds of the ball on different surfaces. I also learned the quickest exit routes just in case Mom heard me break something!

One night during a thunderstorm, I awoke, got out of bed, and walked to the window to watch the rain pelt the backyard with large drops. As the wind swirled the rain across the grass, the lightning illuminated the puddles forming on our muddy basketball court. The temptation was too much for me. I forced opened my bedroom window and crawled out into the downpour. In my bare feet I ran to the muddied ground and began to dribble. The water splashed and the mud splattered the legs of my pajamas as I bounced the ball between my legs and behind my back. After several minutes, I stopped dribbling and lifted the ball toward the sky watching the rain cleanse the mud from it. A huge smile curled across my lips, for I knew if I could dribble under these conditions, I would have no problem on a basketball court.

My theory was quickly confirmed when I took what I'd practiced onto the court at Clemson University. At first the college players were amused to see a little 5'2", ninety-pounder bouncing the ball on the court with such confidence. But it wasn't long before they discovered I was as serious about the game as any of them, and I was ready to take on any of them in a game of one-on-one or horse.

Soon I was challenging my Dad's college players to a game of horse for money. The Clemson players took long shots, and I followed with my modified pistol delivery. My small frame demanded all the strength I could manage to match the twenty-five-footers. I bent down, taking the ball to my right knee, then lunged for the bucket. The shot looked terribly awkward, but the finger pad control, backspin, and follow-through practice paid dividends as the ball ripped through the net more often than not.

At the time Clemson was pretty much a one-horse town and outside basketball there wasn't much for me to do. Movies became my second interest. I went to every Saturday matinee I could, soaking in the fantasy of the big screen. If I wasn't hiding out in the YMCA, I found seclusion in my private world of the movie house and allowed the silver screen to become my main escape from people and situations that made me uncomfortable.

I was quite content sitting in seclusion as the motion picture provided an escape. The empty theater was peaceful, yet still a productive environment for me since I made it a rule to sit on the aisle seat of the first row and dribble the ball during the feature. I bounced the ball on the carpeted aisle to minimize the noise, but since I was usually the only person in the cinema, no one ever complained anyway.

My total dedication to the dream Dad gave me wavered only slightly a couple of times before high school. Once was during the summer when baseball was in the air. I found an old mitt in the closet and coaxed Dad into the backyard to hit me some flies. I eagerly sprinted to the edge of the backyard and took a fielder's stance, my hands on my knees.

"A high one, Pop, a high one!" I shouted, as I spit into my mitt.

Dad rolled his eyes and adjusted his chewing tobacco. An active interest in playing baseball was the last thing he wanted to have me develop. He believed a man could never be a champion in one sport if he wasn't solely dedicated to it.

"Come on Pop! Hit it!" I yelled, impatiently.

He gripped the bat and whispered, "I hope he doesn't choose baseball over basketball." My Dad hated to do it, but he knew he wasn't much of a father if he didn't play baseball with his son. "Here she comes!" he shouted.

My feet shuffled nervously as he swung as hard as he could. The ball shot straight up as if it were fired from a cannon. Even Dad was impressed with the hit as he watched the ball reach its apex and start back to earth. I backed up and positioned myself, keeping my eyes fixed on the baseball. Unfortunately, I was looking directly into the sun and lost sight of the ball. I guess I was used to the larger dimensions of a basketball, because that little baseball dodged my glove, finding its contact point on my forehead. Down I went in a heap, writhing in pain.

Dad ran over and saw a knot the size of a small egg, and the imprint of the baseball's stitches in dark red.

"I got hit by a baseball once. Knocked me out of commission for a week," Dad cautioned.

"Really?" I sniffled, fighting back the tears.

"That's right. Put me in the hospital. That's why I stuck with basketball," Dad answered as he put the bag of ice, which Mother had brought out, on my forehead. Mom exchanged a look with Dad, knowing exactly what he was up to as he casually walked away.

The only other diversion from my dream came when football season rolled around. Dad left nothing to chance this time. He had the eighth grade coach put me in a vulnerable quarterbacking situation. The secret orders were to cream the quarterback. After one pileup and several late hits, I retired my cleats.

To help restore my unwavering love for basketball, Dad knew he had to provide even more challenges. He began by teaching me to balance a broomstick on my finger. With a little agility and coordination plus a lot of concentration, the feat took only a few minutes to master; and before long, I was balancing anything I could pick up: mops, shovels, sticks, anything I could hold with one hand. From that point, Dad took me back to the basketball and showed me how to spin it on my finger. In a couple of weeks I was spinning the ball and before long was able to keep it in a continual spin for several minutes.

I couldn't get enough basketball. When Dad was coaching the Clemson team, I was there. When he went to scout a team, I was there watching every move and listening to every word. We were married to our sport, and together we continued to grow in knowledge and understanding of what basketball could be. I was so close to Dad in his study of the game that he began treating me as if I were an assistant coach. At age thirteen, I identified plays and patterns and made suggestions to Dad as to how he should devise defenses to combat certain offenses, and vice versa. I became a real student of basketball, and this was just the beginning.

Dad's tenure at Clemson was full of ups and downs and the Tigers were a struggling team, but the media were kind to the flashy coach with the crew cut. They were intrigued with the funny guy who "chewed towels and tobacco"—not at the same time, of course. Chewing the edge of a towel throughout the whole game became his habit and trademark on the court. But tobacco was still his constant companion off the court.

Dad surprised everyone in the conference at the end of the 1961–62 season when he took the Clemson team to the finals of the ACC tournament, coaching his squad past perennial powerhouses North Carolina State (67–46) and Duke (77–72).

The final game of the tournament ironically pitted Dad against his old friend Bones McKinney and a strong Wake Forest team, led by forward Len Chappell and a fiery guard by the name of Billy Packer. Dad and his good friend squared off at the scorer's table for their usual conversation and pregame threats. After a couple of jokes, Bones told my Dad he'd have to win this game on his own since Billy Graham was overseas doing a crusade. The Clemson Tigers fought admirably, but lost 77–66.

The years in Clemson, South Carolina, also meant the beginning of high school basketball for me. I was an eighth grader weighing in at just over ninety pounds. When I stretched, I was a notch over 5'2" tall. But long hours of practice, and continual learning from my father helped me overcome such disadvantages and helped prepare me for high school basketball.

Though I was a foot shorter than my teammates, I had the confidence to challenge anyone. And so, the legend of little Pistol Pete began.

9

Pistol Pete

The building had stood there for years. As the large wooden door slowly opened, the creaking hinges sent a squeaking sound through the rafters. When I was thirteen years old I spent most of the year in the old gymnasium of the YMCA. It was my world; my solitude and fortress; my home away from home. Day after day, for hours on end, I practiced shooting, ball handling, dribbling, and passing in the old gym. During the summer months I was almost always alone.

Total dedication to basketball isolated me from most of my friends. But as far as I was concerned, I didn't really need the company unless they were interested in a game of one-on-one. That was rarely the case.

On Saturday morning my routine was off to its normal beginning. I practiced the drills Dad had given me as well as some I was inventing on my own: the ricochet, the bullet ricochet, the pretzel, the space clap, the see-saw, and the punching bag. All these drills improved my quickness and my hand-and-eye coordination; as a result, my confidence was strengthened.

I spent thousands of hours practicing basketball in the YMCA. To break the monotony I attempted anything I could think of to do with a basketball. I began shooting numerous trick shots such as bouncing the ball off the wall and the ceiling, getting it to ricochet into the basket. I was only limited by my imagination.

Whenever Dad saw boredom setting in, his creativity pushed me, eliminating it. He even had me stretch out the passenger side of our car and try to control my dribble as he drove at various speeds. We got the strangest looks from people who saw us. This

75

imaginative escape renewed my interest and kept the daily routine
fun for me.

One afternoon a schoolmate saw me spinning the ball as I stood
in the drugstore soda shop. He walked up and bet me five dollars I
couldn't spin the ball for an hour. Immediately my mind went to
work. Back then I could do a lot with five bucks. A movie cost only a
quarter and popcorn was ten cents. One of the local restaurants
even had a dinner special that included hamburger steak, french
fries, onion rings, biscuits, and all the iced tea I could drink for
ninety-nine cents. My mouth watered just thinking about it.

I took the bet and began spinning the ball. Before long, several
kids gathered around to watch. As the minutes passed, my friends
began to see fatigue setting into my arm and hand. The boy who
made the bet began to gloat, seeing that my index finger was
bleeding. But, before he could start counting his money, I threw
him a curve by switching fingers. That was only the beginning. As
the minutes moved by, I moved the spinning ball from each finger
on my right hand to each finger on my left. When the tips of my
fingers became tender, I spun the ball on my knuckles and thumbs.
In the end I kept the ball in a continual spin for over an hour and
collected the five dollars. Hamburger steak never tasted so good!

I found other challenges off the court, and many were in the local
pool hall. One day I took my twenty-five cent allowance and
entered the pool hall with the confidence of "The Hustler."

Almost always the game was nine ball, and as in anything else I
hated to lose. The rules were simple: twenty-five cents for the first
player who knocked in the five ball, then, another twenty-five
cents for the player who knocked in the ninth and final ball. Some
days I started playing with no money at all. Playing with empty
pockets created even more of a challenge. Having no money left no
room for mistakes and no such thing as losing since I would not be
able to pay the debt.

One of my favorite billiards incidents happened on one of the
days the State Bureau of Investigation sent an agent to investigate
gambling in small establishments such as my favorite pool hall.
The agent had been in several times before, and everyone knew
him by sight and by name. Of course, all betting ceased when the
agent entered the hall.

To my surprise, the agent walked over and began talking to me. He acknowledged the fact that I had a lot of talent and a lot of potential; then he broke the balls. He coolly ran the table as I watched. All the while I just knew he was going to arrest me, but to my surprise the agent merely gave me more tips on how to improve my game. After he slapped in the nine ball, he casually warned me about the evils of gambling. It was an incident that this thirteen-year-old hustler didn't soon forget.

My varsity basketball career began at Daniel High School in Clemson. When I walked onto the court for my first game I heard people laughing and jeering, making remarks about the tiny little guy. I tried to ignore the humiliation, but I wasn't going to be denied. There I stood, a ninety-pound eighth-grader shooting warm-ups with boys who were ten to fourteen inches taller and five years older.

I tried to overcome the embarrassment by resting in the knowledge I would soon be out on the floor displaying my skills. That would surely quiet the crowd, I thought. I also was encouraged by my big brother, Ronnie. He had been a starter all four of his high school years, and he was as cool as a cucumber when he faced a cheering crowd. I wanted to be just like him.

However, my debut was pretty disappointing. Once I passed the ball starting a play I seldom got it back. The senior starters kept the ball from me the entire night. No matter what I did, they wouldn't throw me a pass. I was terribly frustrated after the game and spent most of the night in my bed crying. Dad tried to console me, telling me how he had had to pay his dues when he made his high school team. But nothing he said could take away the pain of not being accepted. Dad realized he hadn't prepared me for this type of disappointment.

My next game was more of the same until the closing seconds of the game. The opposing team held a one point lead as Ronnie and the other seniors moved the ball for the last shot. With the clock running out, I stood open with no one guarding me. They had no reason to guard me—I rarely got the ball. I couldn't have planned it better. I was open and the ball was surprisingly passed to me; without a second thought, I let it fly from my hip. The ball was up and through, and we won the game! Once I heard people clapping for me, I realized I was accepted. It was the first time I had ever gained such approval, and the feeling was great.

A newspaper reporter latched on to the story of the eighth-grader starting on a high school varsity team. During a pregame warm-up he told me I looked like I was drawing a pistol when I launched the ball. The remark was overheard by some players and the nickname "Pistol Pete" stuck.

My reputation spread rapidly, and Daniel High School was known as the team with the little trickster playing guard. Even though the norm was a fundamental bounce or chest pass, the unconventional pass was what people seemed to like and to talk about.

Years with Dad helped prepare me for any situation I encountered on the court. Almost immediately coaches used double coverage on me, which forced me to dribble and pass the ball out of trouble. When I threw a behind-the-back pass the applause began, encouraging me to continue playing the style of basketball I had learned. The spectators liked what they saw and the attendance started to rise. Before long the Daniel High School team became the team to beat in the conference.

The team's success wasn't all my doing, of course. The other players were very gifted, especially a strong forward also named Maravich. Ronnie was my mentor on the court. He also became my protector when jealous opponents took out their frustrations on me, taking advantage of my small stature. At one time Ronnie led the state in technical fouls—mostly due to the retaliation he dished out to those who abused his little brother on the court. Ronnie had a quick temper. He once beat up a fan for throwing ice at me. But he loved me and wanted opposing teams to show me some respect.

Ronnie's protection of me did more for our relationship than any other thing. I know it was strange for him to have his little brother on his team, especially when he could only think of me as the little pest who bugged him at home. But our brotherhood grew stronger as teammates.

Our equality ended once we walked off the court. I looked up to my big brother and wanted to follow in his footsteps as an athlete and a popular kid in town. He was all-state in football and basketball. Unfortunately, the public person I saw wasn't the Ronnie some knew. He had another side: a rebellious side that was successfully hidden from me.

Ronnie demanded a lot of respect from his peers because he was a fighter and very tough. His life was the pool hall and as many girls as he could find. He once skipped so many school days that it took the football coach's pleading and some fancy bookwork to keep him on the team roster. He hated school with a passion, but he loved sports and the glory of winning.

Ronnie kept this dark side from me, leading me to believe he was cool and responsible, when in essence, he was creating mischief everywhere he went, such as the time he bombed the girl's restroom or the time he stole an Edsel. I guess my innocence and Ronnie's cleverness prevented me from seeing the real person he was. I was so naive I never knew Ronnie and some of the players drank bourbon before each game. I just knew Ronnie was the greatest athlete around, and I admired him for it. That was all that mattered to me then. Now, I realize his lack of discipline and rebelliousness kept him from reaching his full potential as an athlete.

The first season was drawing to a close when Daniel High met our main conference rivals for the last game of the year. Newspapers ran articles about the two best teams in the state deciding the conference championship. On that night the gym was packed to the rafters with spectators. Dad and Mom sat in the stands eager to see both their boys bring home the conference banner.

As the game began Dad detected a curiosity in my implementation of the offense. I found myself forcing the ball into bad situations and taking ill-advised shots. Ronnie had complained to me in the past about hogging the ball, and on one occasion he even stole the ball from me during a game just to get a shot.

It was happening again. Ronnie was expected to be in double figures before the night was through, but he was being double teamed and we couldn't get the ball into the pivot for him. I was having the game of my life putting on a dribbling and shooting show that had the fans from both teams on their feet most of the game. With Ronnie covered, I was left open to shoot.

Meanwhile, Ronnie did manage to get a few shots, but only from offensive rebounds. Just before regulation time ended we tied the game and sent it into overtime. Ronnie came to the huddle shouting at me to get the ball inside to him. He was sure he could score inside if he could just get some passes underneath.

We returned to the floor and to an emotionally drained crowd. Dad and Mom were on their feet with the rest of the Daniel High supporters, cheering for their sons and Daniel to win it all.

As I stood near center court, the words of my coach echoed in my head. He wanted us to control the ball and stick to the offense. We exchanged baskets keeping the score deadlocked.

The clock ticked off the final seconds of the overtime period. The winner of this game would surely go on to win the state championship, and I knew it better than anyone. I brought the ball down the court, down by one, to set up the final shot, knowing if we could sink the basket I would have the first championship of my life in my first year playing!

The crowd counted down the time on the clock, "Ten, nine, eight, seven . . ." I dribbled around avoiding my defenders as I heard the crowd screaming, "Shoot! Shoot!" I shot the ball and it headed toward the goal with a beautiful backspin. The Daniel fans held their breath, but the ball bounced off the rim and the final buzzer sounded. Daniel High wouldn't be going to the playoffs. We lost the conference championship, but our opponent went on to easily win the state championship.

I left the gym with tear stains on my face. I was devastated as I took total responsibility for the loss. After one of the most grueling physical and mental battles of my life, the scars were deep. Encouragement from Mom and Dad helped soothe the hurt temporarily, but I had been so close to my dream of a championship season and had let it slip through my fingers. The disappointment and reality of losing destroyed the innocence of the game for me, but my determination to do it all again was unchanged.

10

Growing Pains

Sunday mornings meant attending church for the Maravich family. The days in Aliquippa attending Reverend Anderson's Bible class had left an impression on Dad, and he wanted our family to be well grounded in the teachings of the Scriptures. His faith in God saw him through plenty of rough times, and he sensed the need to expose Ronnie and me to the same inspirations.

Some major problems had to be dealt with, however. Ronnie viewed attending church much the same way he did attending school. He wasn't interested. Being much younger, I had less of a choice in the matter, so when Sunday morning rolled around I was in a pew with the rest of my friends. Unfortunately, attending Sunday school services out of obligation did nothing but emphasize the god I really loved to pay homage to—basketball.

When it came time for the lengthy Bible lesson, my anxiety was almost too much for me to bear. All I could think of were the precious moments being wasted when I could have been playing basketball. I tried my best to make the time pass as I doodled on a piece of paper, but rather than keeping my mind off basketball, I found myself making slash marks on the paper, each one representing a minute lost. All that ran through my mind was the thought that somewhere in Boston, or Philadelphia, or New York someone was on a playground perfecting his basketball skills, and when it came time for earning a scholarship, that kid would have the advantage over me because I was stuck in church!

The more I tried to wipe the thought from my mind, the worse it got. In Sunday school, when the teacher got long-winded and my scratch paper was full of marks, I couldn't help but glare at him with contempt. As he finally neared the end, I poised myself like a sprinter ready to burst out the door.

Once the final prayer ended, I was off like a shot, racing down the aisle and out the back door to the car where my basketball lay waiting for my itching hands. It was a pitiful dependency, and I had clearly become a basketball robot; an addict to a game I assumed would fill my every need.

The older I became, the more I rejected everything but basketball. For a while, I even began rebelling against Dad's instruction. This element of the challenge was one that Dad hadn't taken into account—the wedge being accidentally placed between his son and himself. My rebellion could be blamed in part on the changes adolescence brings, but the dream also provided another direction for my love and attention. The hugs from Mom and advice from Dad became insignificant and childish for a while as I felt it was time to grow up and discover everything on my own.

That summer Dad convinced the athletic director at Clemson that the government was in need of Dad's services in Puerto Rico. In return the job would be good public relations for the school. The athletic director bought this reasoning, and we flew south.

The truth was that Dad needed more money to make ends meet at home. The bill collectors were on his back; and when a Navy contact told him of the opportunity in the Caribbean island, the money was too tempting to ignore. He knew he must take the work to try to get us out of financial difficulties. During the summer Dad racked up an impressive 28–7 record.

When we came home to begin Dad's second year at Clemson, I gained valuable experience when he allowed me to run full court fast break drills with the Clemson players.

My independent spirit was strongly in place as I entered my freshman year at Daniel High School. I knew I had talent and at the time felt I had learned all I could from my father. I had grown a few inches taller, and my shot had a more refined delivery.

All the instruction Dad had given me in the early years proved to be perfectly timed, because the more independent I became, the less I wanted to listen to the man who had taught me everything.

Dad's open window shooting technique was one foundation that remained with me as I entered my maverick high school days. His theory was based on years of studying poor shooting habits in his clinics. As a player took the ball up for a shot, he noticed that one of his eyes often was blocked by the arm that was shooting. But by moving the shooter's hand only a couple of inches Dad was able to give him better depth perception and a better shot.

Dad had applied his theory to me in my early years, instructing me to lift the ball as if I were about to shoot it, then close my left eye. To my surprise my right eye's view of the basket was totally blocked. Dad identified me as a one-eyed shooter.

To reinforce the principle, Dad took some coins from his pocket and told me to close one eye. He then flipped the coins in the air to me one at a time. I dropped half of them, and the lesson was quickly driven home. He explained that with only one eye on the target I had no depth perception. To restore my confidence, he had me open both eyes. He repeated the experiment, and I didn't drop a coin.

Since 1955 Dad and I had invented and refined over forty drills. They had clever names such as crab catch, pendulum swing, the scrambled eggs, flap jack, around the world, and the Pistol Pete draw. Dad wanted to give me more advice and drills to try, but I had stopped listening.

He was frustrated seeing me rejecting his new ideas; but being the unrelenting armchair psychologist, he developed a back door plan of attack.

One morning Dad detected a sluggishness in my attitude as I practiced. He came to the conclusion I was getting burned out doing the same drills day after day. Dad knew all I needed were fresh drills or variations of the old ones; but since I wasn't listening to him, his new plan had to be somewhat deceptive and include the environment in which I was developing the most—the Clemson gymnasium. He took aside his assistant coach, Bobby Roberts, told him how to advise me, and asked him to give me constructive criticism. Dad's ploy worked. I listened patiently to Coach Roberts's comments and implemented the tips immediately.

That same evening Mom and Dad were preparing themselves for dinner as I burst through the back door shouting the praises of Coach Roberts. I had my ball in my hand, so I began demonstrating the things I had been shown. They commended me, telling me I should continue listening to Coach Roberts. After the exhibition I left the kitchen full of excitement. Mom turned to Dad and congratulated him. She knew Bobby had translated all his instructions to me, and the back door plan was successful.

Other factors led to my sudden need for independence. One was the feeling I had been given the responsibility of filling the shoes of my big brother. Ronnie had a colorful reputation of being a renegade in charge of his own destiny at Daniel High, and he was a tough act for me to follow.

Ronnie graduated and in a sense handed me control of the high school team. So as a tribute to him, I made certain I was given Ronnie's old number, 23, when the jerseys were issued.

When I pulled on number 23, I was taller, stronger, and much more aggressive than I had been the previous year. All areas of my game had improved, and I was given a leadership role. I was still lanky, but I used it to my advantage as I zipped left and right, dribbling behind my back and through my legs with ease.

When I scored thirty-five points in one of my freshman games, our conference opponents started scouting us and making plans to shut me down. Fortunately, the long-awaited growth spurt I'd been praying for finally kicked in, and I was even harder to defend. I remember during the tumultuous eighth grade season I went to Dad in tears asking him how I could possibly become a great basketball player if I stayed so short. To pacify my fears, Dad instructed me to hang from the door frame of my bedroom for a few minutes every night. I followed the prescription, and fortunately for Dad, it was time for my most dramatic growth increase. By my sophomore year I had added five inches to my height.

As a sophomore I averaged twenty-one points per game and never failed to give the spectators their money's worth. The more I scored, the louder the applause, and in turn, the more I felt I was being accepted. We didn't play a conservative game, and this kind of game allowed me to use my abilities. The two-hand chest pass was rarely in my nightly repertoire due to the variety of passes I had learned, including my Alley Oop pass to start fast breaks. The first time I zipped a pass between my defender's legs, the ball bounced to a teammate for an easy lay-up. If it hadn't been for the hundreds of hours of practicing passing, I would never have had the confidence to attempt such a thing.

Heavier media attention started, and my name spread around the state. It was quite an adjustment for a quiet, insecure school boy who preferred solitude and quietness.

What people didn't realize was that the Pistol Pete on the court doing all the scoring and play making was only one side of me. Everyone expected a stellar athlete to be "with it" and popular, but in reality I was still painfully shy off the court.

I remember the first party I ever went to, because in many ways it was a turning point in my life. Before that time I was totally committed to basketball. Thoughts of the opposite sex rarely crossed my mind, until my first kiss. My mother persuaded me to go to the party against my will. I was only twelve at the time, and I recall standing on the front porch anxiously awaiting my ride home. I considered the party a total waste of time since it kept me away from playing basketball.

I stared aimlessly down the street hoping that the next beam of headlights would be from my mom's car. Suddenly, out of the house a pretty brown-haired girl approached and asked if I was having a good time. I quietly answered her, and before I knew it she planted a kiss on my lips that made me tingle all the way down to my toes. I almost fell off the porch. From that point on, the distractions in my life suddenly became the attractions.

The next distraction I encountered was the lure of alcohol. When I took my first drink of beer, it seemed pretty innocent. A buddy of mine asked me if I had ever had one.

"No way!" I answered. "If I ever do, it's all over for me!"

"What are you talking about? It won't kill you," he said.

"I know it won't, but my Dad will! He said if I ever drank beer he'd take me out and shoot me with a .45!" I said. "I don't want to die this young. I gotta play basketball."

It may have sounded like I was kidding, but I knew Dad would punish me severely if he ever found out. My buddy just scoffed and kept on me about it. He turned on the peer pressure, and eventually I gave in.

"We'll get a freshman from Clemson to buy it for us, but where can we drink it?" he wondered.

"The Methodist church," I told him. "No one's ever there on Sunday night." I was right. At 9:00 p.m. we sat on the steps of the church, and I had my first taste of beer.

"How do you like it?" my buddy asked me.

"It's great. I don't know why I never tried it before," I answered.

I am convinced that that first drink twenty-five years ago eventually nearly killed me. I realized later a real friend would never have asked me to make such a choice. Alcohol is a drug, and 70 percent of all kids today are pressured into trying drugs. A real friend is someone who cares for you and will never commit you to an immoral decision. But, like most things, even peer pressure is made up of choices. I didn't have to take that first drink, but I chose to do it because I wanted desperately to fit in. No one forced me.

Though I attempted to withdraw from my dad's wisdom and his coaching, I was still subject to him and his personal decisions. After my record-setting 483 points as a high school sophomore, and Dad's six seasons at Clemson, he pulled up stakes and moved the family. Independent, or not, I was headed to Raleigh, North Carolina, where Dad had taken an assistant coaching job under Everett Case.

My dad received a lot of criticism for leaving a head coaching job in the ACC to take an assistant coaching position in the same conference, but economics overruled once more. He received a thirty-five hundred dollar raise at North Carolina State, and Needham-Broughton High School in Raleigh received a junior transfer for their basketball program.

11

Rewards

When Mom and Dad moved us to Raleigh, North Carolina, in 1963, the future looked brighter than ever. Though Dad left his head coaching job at Clemson, the deal he struck with North Carolina State contained ingredients that seemed to make all the bad decisions in the past easier to swallow.

Everett Case, the coach at NC State, tracked down Dad through a series of phone calls and finally found him at his moonlighting job in Puerto Rico. The message was short but very sweet for my dad. Case wanted him to work under him for two or three years, then Case would announce his resignation to the university, at which time the program would then be placed in the capable hands of my dad, a man groomed by Coach Case himself. Case left it to Dad to sell the idea to the college administration.

The offer sounded good over the phone, so Dad set up a meeting in August, when his season in Puerto Rico ended. At the end of the summer, he entered the athletic director's office and placed the terms of his employment on the table. He told the A.D. that he wanted a six-year contract; three years as assistant coach under Coach Case, then three years as head coach after Case's retirement. The athletic director was surprised at the demand, and his reply was negative. He was certain the school could never agree to such a lengthy contract under the stated terms. Dad was then sent to the chancellor to plead his case.

"I want a six-year deal. Three under Case, and three as head coach when Everett retires." Dad said boldly as the chancellor reviewed his resumé. The room was quiet as the chancellor jotted a few words on the paper. Dad kept his stiff upper lip. The fact that he still had the head coaching position back in Clemson if things didn't work out gave him the confidence he needed to make his demands. He was employed with or without the new job.

The chancellor cleared his throat and sat back in his leather chair. "Okay, what else?" he replied calmly.

Dad was taken aback for a moment, unprepared for the quick acceptance. "That'll do, chancellor," he smiled. And the agreement was made.

That quiet moment in the chancellor's office may have seemed insignificant at the time, but across town at Needham-Broughton High School, Dad's decision had a profound effect on my life and influenced the complexion of a growing high school basketball program.

The Needham-Broughton Caps were in the Eastern 4A Conference; a conference considered the most powerful and most respected in the state. Atlantic Coast Conference universities had come to the Caps for years to gather quality talent for their athletic programs. When I arrived at my new high school, the coach claimed to have another all-American in the works. All I knew was I was eager to get started and prove myself in the new surroundings.

I had grown to be nearly six feet tall, and the Caps just happened to be hurting for a point guard. Their season a year earlier had been disappointing, ending with an 8–13 record. But this season they returned four starting senior lettermen and their prospects were good, especially if they could adequately fill the gap in the line-up. I was ready to prove their need had been met. The coach gave me a lot of responsibility, counting on me to spearhead the squad.

The situation was perfect for me, except for one factor still haunting me—my stature. My weight was still hovering at 130 pounds. I didn't have the bulk to adequately protect my body. In no way was my offensive scoring affected by the size, but my stamina sometimes was. Games that demanded an unrelenting defense took its toll on my slight frame, and my energy could run thin in the final quarter.

Opposing teams made it a point to capitalize on my slight structure. With a lack of muscle and meat for protection, an elbow thrown into my ribs bent me over and had me gasping for breath. Many nights I was knocked to the floor by an overzealous player or deliberately fouled by an opponent upset by my scoring binge. The hotter my shooting, the hotter my opponents seemed to get under the collar.

As a result of the abuse, I developed my own form of retaliation. If the man guarding me became too aggressive, I had a knack of drawing the foul by falling or stumbling backward, convincing the referee that an infraction had occured. My acting skills might not have convinced a theater critic, but it was adequate enough to make me a constant visitor to the free-throw line.

Needham-Broughton turned things around, ending our year with a 19–4 record. I had never been so beaten and bruised, but my basketball savvy was sharpened even more.

If bodily harm was my physical obstacle, learning how to handle a loss was my mental obstacle. I never fully recovered from the disappointments at Daniel High School, and it seemed that every loss still loomed larger than all the wins combined. I found it increasingly hard to sleep at night with the thought of defeats on my mind.

Dad considered my dark moods and lack of sleep as natural byproducts of a champion's dedication to winning. He remembered trying to instill that characteristic in me when we played in the backyard in Clemson. When Dad let me beat him in a game of one-on-one, he kicked his toe in the dirt and put on an entire act to show me how horrible it felt to lose. Whether it was a contributing factor or not, the fact remained that, in my mind, a loss was totally unacceptable.

Needham-Broughton reached the state quarter-finals, and the Caps managed to squeak past Wilmington. With the first win under our belts, I believed we were about to land our first championship.

In the semi-finals, our game went into double overtime, but it ended on a very controversial play. One of our players, Jimmy Broadway, threw up a desperation shot from half court as the buzzer sounded. We were down by one, and our hopes were riding on the success of his shot. The ball miraculously found its mark, and we began our celebration. But, as the official from our conference called the shot good, the official from the opposing conference negated the basket, and we were defeated.

Though the crowd and the media praised our performance, we

left the arena despondent and blaming the official for the loss. I should have celebrated the Caps 19–4 record, but all I could think of were the stupid mistakes I had made to contribute to the defeat that lost our chance at the title. For months after the season, I was haunted by the championship slipping from our hands.

Once summer arrived, I could finally put the season behind me and start to relax. Since the time of my first drink on the church steps, pleasures other than basketball began to creep into my life.

I remember one particular night my buddies and I went out for a good time. I drank way too much and passed out. I wasn't too concerned because I assumed I would be staying out all night. Instead I was awakened by my buddies in the driveway of my house. I couldn't believe they would bring me home in my condition because they knew my dad!

It was about one o'clock and the front door was open. When I approached the screen door, there Dad was, waiting. He looked at me and said, "You're drunk! Get in here!"

He took a swing at me and I ducked. In a flash, I ran up the stairs to my room for refuge. He stormed after me but as usual, Mom followed and grabbed him.

"I'm gonna kill you!" Dad screamed. His blood was boiling, and he was nearly out of control; but somehow Mom managed to cool him off and save me.

Early the next morning, I sneaked out of the house at 5:00 a.m. I wasn't trying to escape, but rather set myself to working around the house. I mowed the lawn, raked the leaves, and even washed Dad's car in an attempt to smooth things over and get back in his good graces.

As usual around 8:45, Dad walked out of the house on his way to work. He saw me and shouted, "You're grounded for six weekends, and if you leave this place, I'll shoot you!"

I thought his punishment was too severe. He knew the worst thing he could do was keep me confined to the house on weekends. But, I began to think about what I had done that night, and I realized his punishment wasn't severe enough.

For as long as I can remember, summertime also meant attending a basketball camp with Dad. In North Carolina, I attended Everett Case's Wolfpack's basketball camp and polished my skills with college athletes as well as professionals who were invited to instruct.

To my advantage I always had access to the Wolfpack gym and players, and because of it I became a constant fixture on campus. As at Clemson the college team at NC State seemed to like having me around. When a game of horse began, they knew all holds were barred. I knew the quickest way to win the bets and take their money was to begin my trick shots.

What friends I did have seemed to be the college guys. They made me feel welcome by asking me to join them for burgers after practice. With all the media attention and public recognition, they helped me handle it by treating me as a buddy. I was still painfully shy, but after a few beers I loosened up.

While I was maturing in my game at Needham-Broughton, things for Dad took an interesting turn. He and Mom had a beautiful baby enter their lives. They named my little sister Diana Marie. Not only did Dad have the new responsibility of a child to raise, but after one year Coach Case's long-term plans were brought to a sudden halt when he became ill. He was unable to carry out his duties as a coach, and though it was a great loss for the university and its athletic program, Case had provided well for the institution to which he had given so much. He left them with a healthy program as well as one of the best coaches in the East, my dad.

Dad had a spectacular first year as the Wolfpack's head coach. His iron fist ruled the bench when his team took the floor. He chewed more towels during the games than ever before. Although his team lacked talent, they didn't lack heart. They brought excitement to a city that had been looking for another championship team. And as I knocked down scoring records with the Caps, Dad reached milestones for North Carolina State, taking his club into the ACC tournament final against Wake Forest.

With a 21–5 record to his credit, Dad entered the NCAA tournament riding high, only to be humbled by a talented Princeton team lead by a kid named Bill Bradley. Dad took the seven point loss pretty hard, but found some solace in the consolation bracket when the Wolfpack trounced Jack Ramsey's St. Joseph's number three rated team in the country.

91

Both of us wrote our names in North Carolina history books with one big year. We weren't on the same court, but it felt as though we had done it all together.

Dad took his team to the ACC finals two years in a row. The second year NC State dropped the final game to Duke in overtime. Dad's 40–12 record in two years as head coach was nothing to be ashamed of.

I grew six inches between my junior and senior years. As a 6'4" senior at Needham-Broughton, I was the only starter returning from the 19–4 team. The responsibility fell upon me to be the leader of an inexperienced team. It seemed when I was hot, the team was hot, and when I cooled off for a time, the team seemed to follow suit. Though I was averaging thirty-two points per game, the weight of responsibility at times annoyed me; and I remember letting Dad know about it.

"Everybody's out there lookin' at me . . . waiting for me to do it all," I complained one evening.

"Then, do it! You have the talent," Dad replied, half angry and half reassuring.

"They'll call me a hot dog, and you know it," I continued.

"Well, that's their problem, now, isn't it? You use all the abilities you have and play your game. If you have to use deceptive passes like behind the back or between your legs, let your instincts take over. Do it and stop worrying about what people will say!" Dad growled.

These discussions were the norm as our unique father-son relationship continued to grow. Mom detected the changes as Dad and I treated each other more like coach and player rather than dad and son. Sometimes at home she was subjected to entire evenings of strategy sessions and chalk talks. She kept the hot coffee and ice cream coming as we bantered about basketball philosophy. I could score thirty points in a crucial game, but Dad would point out all the mistakes I made hoping I would not repeat them again. Perhaps the mistake had been a turnover or a poorly timed shot; whatever it was, it seemed to override any of the positive points.

A gray area was created between father and son, coach and player. The combination resulted in a strong bond of mentor and protégé. I knew my dad had more basketball knowledge in his little finger than most coaches combined; and though it was difficult living under the same roof with Dad, I was aware of the tremendous advantage I had over other young players.

Though I was skinny as a rail, I tried to use my height and floor speed to penetrate as never before. A great deal of my scoring came as a result of dribbling through traffic, driving along the baseline, and shooting reverse lay-ups. By my senior year my hook shot was true from both sides, which gave me even more dimension. Still, the championship I longed for remained elusive. In my senior year the Caps finished with a dismal 8–13 season.

The only thing that rivaled the agony of losing was the disappointment of missing a game due to injury. I learned the necessity of playing with pain early in my career. In one particular game I had to overcome a swollen foot caused from a torn arch. Despite doctor's orders at half time, I persisted and eventually won permission to continue the game. My foot was taped securely, and a shoe several sizes larger than mine was fitted over the mound of tape and wrap.

Our rival Fayetteville and their superstar 7'0" Rusty Clark were dominating the game. I limped onto the floor and received a large ovation from the crowded auditorium.

I overcame the pain and dragged my foot behind me up and down the court for the last half. Only ball handling and some creative passing kept the players from taking total advantage of my crippled condition. Somehow I managed to drive the lane, and with some adjustments, managed to rework my jump shot. Of course my game was much less aerial since leaping and vertical jumps were out of the question. Unfortunately, not even a forty-five point performance was enough to help the Caps beat Fayetteville.

I ended with a better than average two years at Needham-Broughton: a 32-point average per game my senior year; 1,185 points in two seasons; thirty-two times over 20 points in both seasons; thirteen times over 30 points in two years; and six times over 40 points in two seasons.

After graduation Dad and I decided I should attend prep school for a year before subjecting myself to a college basketball program and the rigors of university level academics. My preoccupation with basketball had affected my performance in the classroom. Dad suggested Edwards Military Academy in Salemburg, North Carolina, as a warm-up before college life, and Mom agreed. I had grown to 6'4" but Dad knew I would be beaten physically if he pushed me on into college and I went up against players on the university level, especially in the highly competitive Atlantic Coast Conference.

Again, Dad was correct in his judgment. Edwards helped put a little more strength in my body, as well as discipline me some more in the classroom. The basketball program was also a plus. We were a fast-break oriented team.

One morning Mom opened the newspaper to show Dad the sports page. The headlines read, "50? Maravich?" She assured Dad he had made the right decision in sending their boy to prep school. Dad took the fifty-point game as confirmation as well. He felt I would be the most sought after freshman in the entire country when schools started opening the scholarship purses the following year.

The highlight of my year at Edwards was the night I played against the freshman team of NC State. The newspapers hyped the game pitting Maravich against Maravich. Though Dad coached only the varsity it made for good publicity. During the game I pumped in thirty-three points and led the team to a 91–57 blowout. Dad just smiled, feeling the future for both of us would become even brighter.

Dad envisioned a lot in regard to his career and my future, and one of his dreams included the opportunity to coach me. He had a gift of unleashing an athlete's talent, encouraging him to use his strong points for the good of the entire team.

An offer from Louisiana State University tempted Dad to begin his vision. When he met secretly with LSU officials to negotiate a contract, Dad had never felt so tense. The palms of his hands were sweaty as he swallowed hard and laid his terms on the table. The situation wasn't new, but he had never asked for such an enormous amount of money. The figure kept swirling in his head as he eyed the athletic director. *If they'll go for this, I can get my family out of debt, once and for all,* he thought. He felt he owed it to his family.

The LSU official waited patiently for Dad's request. Dad was afraid the sum was too high and that he would embarrass himself and blow the job. But after another moment of anxiety, he blurted out his terms. "I need fifteen thousand dollars and a five-year contract," he said. Dad waited, expecting a resounding "No." But, to his surprise, the terms were accepted without argument.

With the deal secure, he traveled back to North Carolina and told his athletic director he was talking with LSU, and that an offer had been made. He tested the waters to see if NC State would come up with more money, never letting it be known that he had already taken the LSU job.

When no counter offer was made by NC State, Dad was resigned to make the move to the Bayou country. To his surprise, he was in more demand than he realized. Before he could relax with his decision to travel to Baton Rouge, the owner of the Baltimore Bullets contacted Dad, wanting him to coach his NBA club. Dad could hardly believe what was happening.

Dad suddenly realized his negotiations with LSU were a Sunday picnic in comparison to sitting across from an owner of a professional franchise. He was playing hardball with the big boys; high rollers in the world of basketball business. Again, sweat formed in the palms of his hands as he mulled over his demands.

"I need $100,000 . . . and a six year, no-cut contract," Dad said, knowing he had nothing to lose. He could hardly believe the words actually came out of his mouth. Dad had just asked for more per month than he was making in a year. The moment made him lightheaded, and he hoped the owner would say something quickly. He did. A six-year deal was out of the question.

Dad countered, arguing the fact that he knew if the Bullets lost the first few games he would be fired in a heartbeat. He needed time to build the team; create public interest in the franchise; bring in great talent. Dad finished his speech by admitting he could really use the money, but he had his pride, and he wouldn't jeopardize his family's future. He had to have the no-cut deal.

Dad ultimately took the LSU offer, and the Bullets' new coach lost his job after the first few games. In regard to job security, Dad made the right decision. In my opinion at the time though, he needed his head examined.

The news of his surprising decision came to me as I stood in the

Pittsburgh airport. I was bound for one of my summer clinics when I spotted a familiar figure walking toward me in the distance. I took off my sunglasses to get a better look and to my surprise it was Dad. He had a solemn look on his face.

"Dad, what is it? What are you doing here?" I asked.

"I want you to sign something," he said, calmly.

"What's this?" I asked, glancing at the document. I read the first few lines, then smiled. "Louisiana State? What is this, a joke, Dad?"

Dad checked his quick temper and handed me a pen. "Sign it," he said. "It's a grant-in-aid. I took the job at LSU, and you're coming with me."

I was flabbergasted. "No way! You gotta be kiddin' me, Dad. LSU? That's a football school! Dad, you wanted me to play ball for West Virginia, and that's what I'm gonna do!" I retaliated.

"You're coming with me!" he shouted.

"No!" I replied.

The moment was intense as two strong-willed Serbs had their first powerful face-off. I found it inconceivable that I was being asked to make such a move. And Dad wasn't about to let his son defy him. This was all a part of his plan—a part of the dream. With all the forcefulness he could muster, Dad looked me in the eye and delivered an ominous ultimatum.

"Sign the paper, son . . . or don't ever come home again," he said in a voice that could sharpen steel.

Not since I came home drunk had I seen my father like this. Through every heated argument we ever had, I could always detect a hint of love and compromise; but now it was as if I had come face to face with a total stranger—a man who could accept no compromise whatsoever. What I didn't realize was the fact that Dad had just given the best performance of his life.

After what seemed like an eternity, I finally gave in, took the paper, and signed it. I was full of mixed emotions. On one hand I loved my dad more than life itself; but on the other hand, my life was suddenly out of my control and thrown in a completely new direction.

As Dad turned and walked away, I watched him and wondered how my goals could ever be met. Had my dream of a championship been dashed by the very man who instilled the dream in my heart? What could he be thinking? Every move in my life had been based on the trust I had in him.

I picked up my gym bag and started down the terminal hallway several yards behind him. All I could think of was the blind trust I had in him and the hope our dream would one day be fulfilled.

As usual, Dad had a plan. He felt no other coach in the country would allow me to use my talents to my full potential. After teaching and watching me develop, he desired nothing more than to coach me.

He wanted to take the game of basketball and elevate it to a level of excitement and artistry that he had first dreamed possible forty years earlier in the winter snow of Pennsylvania.

The fulfillment of his dream would be for us to do it together.

BOOK THREE
THE HEIR OF APPROVAL
———— 12 ————

The Cow Palace

The campus of Louisiana State University is picturesque, complete with lush green lawns and buildings that reflect the pride of the Old South. The university is the heartbeat of the city's activities, even though Baton Rouge is the capital of the state. LSU dominates the minds of the citizens, especially when fall is in the air and football season begins. This Southeastern Conference powerhouse has spawned some of the greatest football players in the country: Y. A. Tittle, Jim Taylor, Billy Cannon, Mel Branch, Jerry Stovall, and others.

In 1966, Jim Corbett, LSU's energetic athletic director, lured Pop to Baton Rouge. It was Corbett who convinced my dad to take on another rebuilding program and create some excitement in a school that had suffered through years of apathy toward basketball. Not since the days of superstar Bob Pettit back in the 1950s had LSU supported their basketball team.

Dad wasn't looking for another rebuilding challenge when he first interviewed for the LSU position, but he needed more pay. He was still in debt and having to borrow a hundred dollars a month from the NC State football coach just to pay monthly utilities. Dad didn't tell Corbett this information. He didn't have to. Jim Corbett wanted the best coach he could find, and he knew my dad was his man.

Corbett was well aware of Dad's philosophy and approach to the game. He knew my dad always coached a basketball team as if the world's championship were on the line, whether it was the Navy teams or Aliquippa High School. His approach to the fundamentals and to basketball strategy was the same; be as creative as possible, and use the players' capabilities to their fullest. Dad would use this same approach in the bayou, and Jim Corbett banked on it.

Corbett informed the whole town that one of the finest coaches in the country was coming to captain the Tigers, and to top it off, he was bringing his son with him. Unfortunately, the community was so buried in football tradition that this news received a collective yawn. Maybe if I had been a halfback they would have noticed, but no one cared about basketball. It was considered a noncontact sport for softies who were a little light in their loafers.

When Dad went to LSU for his first official tour, the man who had asked him to come wasn't there. Jim Corbett had died of a sudden heart attack, and the school was mourning his loss. The job of orienting Dad to his new surroundings fell on the shoulders of one of the LSU assistants, Jay McCreary.

McCreary was a good company man, and he did his best to conceal the negatives as he drove my dad around the sprawling campus. At the time, Dad didn't think much about it as his tour guide accelerated the car and cruised past the John M. Parker Coliseum. He would discover later that a walking horse show had all rights to the Coliseum until two weeks before Dad would debut his Tiger team. His practice sessions would have to take place in a high school gym with a short floor.

Indifference such as this seemed to spark the drive in Dad to want to succeed all the more. The disappointment would have destroyed a lesser man, but Dad had a long history of creating a great deal from very little. When he had accepted the coaching position at Davis and Elkins the school still had no gymnasium. Dad demanded to know why they were still in the dark ages. When the athletic director told him only thirty-five dollars remained in the athletic fund, Dad borrowed a tractor and cleared some ground by himself. Then he had the local paper run headlines: "Ground Broken For New Gymnasium." Dad begged every retired carpenter, plumber, and masonry man he could find to help him, and with the assistance of eager students he had a five-thousand-seat auditorium built.

But that was Elkins, West Virginia. At LSU Dad would need to contend with a facility he couldn't use until the season was about to begin.

One way to get basketball in the minds of his new audience and build the program would be a full media blitz in Baton Rouge. Before Mom and Dad moved south, he began the hype about bringing the excitement of basketball back to LSU. The media listened. After all, here was one of the hottest coaches in the United States spouting promises of great things to come. He even announced the arrival of his number one recruit, Pistol Pete Maravich, a "superstar on the horizon." His optimism was appreciated, but bragging about me was all the critics needed to begin the ridicule and start a father and son controversy.

When I came to town, there were no brass bands and no ticker tape. Football was in the air; and as far as Louisiana was concerned, that was all that mattered. The basketball team practiced unnoticed in the high school gymnasium.

To make matters worse, Dad had to face the fact that his Tigers were toothless and would no doubt be mauled through the year. His only hope was to survive the year and trust that the Pennsylvania imports he had gathered would gain some respect on the freshman team.

The first season was a nightmare. Out of the twenty-six games scheduled, Dad tasted victory three forgettable times. The experience was horrible for him; he had never coached through a more frustrating season. Everything he tried was a dismal failure, giving the LSU fans more reason to say, "I told you so." He unwillingly fueled the argument that basketball at LSU would always play second fiddle to the football program. Dad had a struggle to keep his attitude out of the gutter as his team lost night after night.

The failures on the court took their toll on home life as Dad worked long hours trying to salvage the season. He had always assumed Mom would be loving and supportive regardless of his success or failure on the basketball court. But after years of living with basketball, she was beginning to bend under the weight. When Dad came home in the evenings he found her uninterested in the happenings at school and also uninterested in trying to keep the home and family in order. The years of being the stabilizer had worn her down, and she began aging far beyond her years.

During the dismal 1966–67 season it seemed Mom was always out of energy and feeling ill. Some nights Dad had to come home and cook, clean, and do laundry after the fourteen-hour day at school. In a time when he needed her support more than ever, she wasn't available to him. The load on his shoulders was almost too much to bear.

On the flipside of all the negative happenings in 1966–67, a phenomenon unfolded before each of the varsity games. Before the season word got around on campus that Coach Maravich's boy would start all the freshman games. The stories of the hotshot from North Carolina were widespread, but skepticism was still the norm because of the attitude toward basketball at LSU. But skepticism didn't keep the curiosity seekers from buying their tickets to see the "Baby Bengals" take the floor for their first game of the season.

The smell of livestock, mingled with popcorn and cigarette smoke, filled the air in the John M. Parker Coliseum. The removable floor was back in place, covering the spot where dirt and manure lay two weeks earlier. The Cow Palace, as it was more commonly known, was set for my college debut.

At 6'4" and 165 pounds soaking wet, I came onto the court. A skeptical spattering of applause bounced around the arena as the freshman team took their warm-ups. We figured we would have to perform better than ever to win over the apathetic crowd. Before the night was over, the fans got totally behind us and put a charge in me. In my debut I managed to pour through fifty points and dump off eighteen assists as we coasted to victory.

I'd been waiting for this night. I passed behind my back, through my legs, and over my shoulders. In one night I tried to turn all the basketball skeptics into disciples, exposing them to a basketball game elevated from the normal sluggish, controlled tempo to a wide-open, catch-us-if-you-can style that our young team quickly installed.

Before long, crowds showed up early for the hottest tickets in town. The young Tigers starred in a show that featured a new plot line every night, but ended the same—another win. The LSU freshman team managed to light a spark that set fire to the campus, the city, and the Southeastern Conference, winning seventeen straight games.

LSU wasn't the University of West Virginia as I had always

imagined, but it was big-time basketball. I was comfortable playing full throttle in Baton Rouge.

A few games into the season, Dad began to wish the freshman games were scheduled after his varsity games because we started packing the Coliseum. Eight thousand students and the local fans nearly knocked down the doors to get in to the first game of the night; and after the Baby Bengal Show, they nearly knocked down the doors to get out. LSU campus security directed more traffic between games than they did after the main contest.

My life changed rapidly. People wanted to know everything they could about me. I answered the only way I knew how. I was a simple guy with a love for the game of basketball; and thanks to great coaching and thousands of hours of practicing the fundamentals, I had managed to become good at it.

When people implied that Dad had made me into a star, I made certain Dad got the coaching credit; but practicing all those hours was something only I could do. I was quick to keep that straight when the media raised accusations of favoritism.

I kept my answers brief and honest when I talked to reporters. Some of their questions were unbelievable. They asked everything they could think of including the origin of my floppy socks.

"I was going to play ball with a friend, Bob Sanford, and I forgot my socks; so I borrowed a pair of old thick gray work socks from him. They were a little large and drooped over my shoes. I had always felt slow because of my big feet, but the floppy socks covered half my shoes and made my feet look smaller and somehow it made me feel faster. I know it's a psychological thing, but I've been wearing them ever since," I answered quickly.

"Are they a good luck charm, Pistol?" one reporter asked.

"I guess so. But they're also comfortable," I told him.

Another trademark I acquired was the mop-top hair style. It was a reflection of the maverick spirit I inherited from my brother, Ronnie. I enjoyed the longer hair styles the Beatles made popular in the 1960s, and decided to wear my hair much longer than the normal short styles. At the time I could relate to a gifted athlete like Joe Namath who wanted sports to be unpredictable and fun. I believed a player should bring his own personality and excitement to his sport, otherwise athletics would be filled with robots all marching to the same drummer.

When I was a freshman, we weren't allowed to play on the varsity team; but the year proved to be a good warm-up for the following three years. I managed to score over fifty points in six different games and reached a personal high of sixty-six against an independent Baton Rouge team. My average after seventeen games was over forty-three points a game when we met our final foes of the year, a scrappy Tennessee team eager to shut down the new kids in the South.

The Volunteers played their usual slow down tempo game, holding me to just thirty points. With the score standing at Tennessee 75 and LSU 73, a foul in the final seconds sent me to the foul line to tie the game. In a one-and-one situation, I approached the line with confidence and sank the first basket. Then, with the crowd silent I shot the second charity shot. The ball rolled around the rim and dropped out. Time ran out and there went our perfect season.

Still unable to handle such a loss, I disappeared for several hours after the game. I needed time alone to deal with the disappointment. Dad and the guys later discovered I had left the gym and walked the two miles back to the hotel.

Losing was like a knife in my heart. Inside, I knew I wasn't much of a sport if I couldn't take a loss once in a while, but I had conditioned myself for so long to be only a winner so anything less was unacceptable. The Tennessee game was a particular personal disaster since I felt I had let down my team, the fans, the school, my Dad, and of course myself. All I could think of was a blemished record: 17–1, and I considered the one loss all my fault. The fact that I was double and triple teamed the entire night was no excuse.

The year taught me more lessons, though accepting a loss wasn't one of them. Dad saw the toll the year had taken on me and thought another summer of camps and clinics would get me away from things that reminded me of the blemished finale.

Since high school I had performed a clinic called "Homework Basketball," later known as "Showtime." My dad saw the pleasure I received while demonstrating techniques we had both developed when I was a boy. The clinic was broken into five segments:

shooting, passing, ball handling, dribbling, and spinning. The clinic was instructional and entertaining.

I was scheduled to perform for a group in California. It would be a long trip from Baton Rouge, but the drive across country was part of the escape therapy Dad prescribed.

A friend and I began the long car ride. On our way the discussions ranged from the Vietnam war to race riots, to girls and more girls, and of course, basketball. The trip turned into one long party as we drank one beer after another and sang Beatles and Rolling Stones songs as loud as we could. But best of all, it was a much needed escape from reality. For the first time in months I was away from the trappings and pressure of college basketball. It felt good.

As we got closer to California, I handled the driving duties and my partner unfolded the road map, trying to focus his bleary eyes on the lines and numbers. Unable to overcome the alcohol, he threw the map in the back seat and closed his eyes. When he came to, I was pulling the car into the drive of our destination, the headquarters of Campus Crusade for Christ.

I noticed groups of people sitting in circles all over the grounds. It didn't take long to realize they were involved in some sort of religious function, and I had no interest whatsoever in getting religious.

A very strange three days followed. On the last day a man named Bill Bright spoke, and I felt obligated to stay. His talk reminded me of the days my parents forced me to spend in church—days that robbed me of time practicing basketball. I got upset and irritated as we sat there, but oddly enough my buddy's attention was held by the simple message Bright gave regarding salvation through God's Son, Jesus. When he finished speaking he invited anyone who had never given their life to Jesus Christ to come and speak with a counselor. When I saw my friend start to stand, I grabbed him.

"Are you out of your mind?" I whispered forcefully. "You're not giving in to all this crap, are you?"

"For the first time in my life, I understand what it's all about, Pete. This isn't religion, man, it's a relationship," he replied.

I couldn't believe my ears. I thought, how could anyone fall for something so stupid. I could see it now—two thousand miles back home in the car with a Jesus freak!

105

As he walked toward the counselors, I played it cool and bowed my head, not wanting to draw any attention to myself. I had played this game before in my parents' church, and I knew the invitation would end soon and I could breathe easier again.

I tried to disregard what I was feeling deep inside as I looked up and saw my friend praying with a young counselor. I started thinking about my own relationship with God. I didn't have much of one since my whole life had been spent worshiping basketball. As I sat waiting nervously, I remembered how I had once prayed that I could reach the goals my dad and I had set for the scholarship, the million dollar pro contract, and most of all, the championship ring. I had reached the first plateau, having proved myself worthy of a college scholarship. I only had two more hurdles to leap.

I wondered if God had really answered my prayer about the scholarship, or I had just been lucky. Regardless, the thought of believing in Jesus Christ and turning my life over to him made me uneasy. *Why bring God into all this*, I thought. *Man, if I get serious about God, and Jesus Christ, I'll have to give up everything! Look at these people, all they do is sit around and sing and read the Bible. They'll never amount to anything. I got things to do with my life. I have goals for me!* The thoughts raced through my head until the meeting broke up.

In the most important moment of my friend's life I remember wanting to keep him from making the decision, just because I was afraid of what such a decision would do to *my* life. I wanted to keep him where he was and in a sense rob him of his salvation.

The next day we left California for Louisiana having never held the clinic. And to this day I'm not sure how we were scheduled to be there. Campus Crusade certainly didn't want a basketball clinic.

The ride home was just as I had expected. My friend drank none of the beer, he just kept reading a Bible he had been given at the Campus Crusade headquarters. To my chagrin, he burst out reading a passage of Scripture every few minutes. "It goes on to say, 'For God did not send His Son into the world to condemn the world, but that the world through Him might be saved.' Can you dig that, Pete?" he said, his voice cracking with excitement.

I took my eye off the road and lowered my mirrored sunglasses. He looked back and smiled. Before another Scripture could be quoted, I turned up the radio.

What was supposed to be a nice get away turned into a trip that made me more anxious and unsettled than ever. When I returned to Baton Rouge, all the old thoughts were back in my head. As my friend quoted Scriptures, I remembered the 124 assists I had on the year, wishing I would have had one more to win the Tennessee game. But, there would be next year . . . in the big time.

With varsity basketball on the horizon I found myself one step closer to the next goal and nothing, not even God, I thought, could stop me!

13

The War

A reporter interviewed me when I was twelve years old and ended the interview with a question about my future. I sat up boldly and stated as a matter of fact what the future held.

"I'm gonna continue to play basketball to the best of my ability," I started. "Then, I'll get a scholarship to play college ball . . . then, I'll play in the pros and be on a team that wins a championship ring—oh, yeah, and they'll pay me a million dollars!"

For a long moment of silence, the reporter tried to suppress his smile. But, before I knew it, he was laughing. I had no idea what was so funny. When the reporter finally caught his breath he explained to me the realities of professional sports. He said the odds of getting a scholarship were bad enough, but making the pros would be like lightning striking twice in the same place. And, as for the million dollars, I could forget it. Good professionals might make twenty thousand dollars.

One thing I hadn't predicted was the effect basketball could have on people as well as the economy. In gate receipts alone, LSU could consider construction plans they had regarding a better facility for the Tigers. The LSU administration was forced to cut off season ticket sales at four thousand in order to give more people a chance to buy a seat. Basketball was alive and well in pigskin country.

Merchants in Baton Rouge felt the impact on their business as basketball brought attention to the capital city. For years shop owners gauged their fiscal health by the activity generated by football season. Restaurants, motels, gas stations, and taverns loved to see the bulging wallets of the out-of-towners as they filled the community for the games on the gridiron. But now, LSU and the southern Louisiana region embraced another sport that would bring revenue and excitement to the basketball-starved South.

Even hardware stores benefited from fathers and sons caught up in the frenzy of roundball. Backboards, rims, and nets were ordered and sold like hotcakes. Backyard goals began to spring up like dandelions in yards and alleys all over the state. Children discovered basketball no longer had to be a methodically controlled contest, limited to a mediocre shot selection.

The new Tigers created an enthusiasm for basketball that warmed the hearts of high school coaches all over the southern states. They loved the interest Dad and his Tigers generated in the high school programs, though students had to be reminded that our showmanship and game strategies didn't just start happening when he arrived at LSU. Despite the coaches' warnings, young players started attempting things on the court they had witnessed while watching Tiger games.

My life changed dramatically in just one year. During the basketball season of 1967–68, maturity was hurled at me. I had longed to play on the varsity as a freshman, but in the days before four-year eligibility, I had to settle for only three years of top-level competition. When I entered my sophomore year, I started competing on the varsity level where scoring and assist records that had stood for years waited to be broken.

In my first three games as a sophomore, I scored 141 points. The national media began their stories about my pursuit of Frank Selvey's scoring average of 43.6 points per game.

This sudden leap to fame was a lot to handle. I had to balance my life between the insecure person I was and the carefree college prankster and athlete I wanted to be. Added to that, representing LSU everywhere I went carried more responsibility.

As a personal rule I wouldn't leave the arena after a game until every autograph seeker got my signature, which sometimes meant a two-hour delay getting home. I must admit I never really understood why people wanted autographs in the first place; I guess people looked to me as a hero. Webster defines a hero as a man noted for his special achievements. *Hero* is also defined as a long sandwich. Since a lot of people called me a hot dog during my career, either definition may have been the reason people wanted my autograph.

At times I detected the groupies gathering at practices to sneak a peek. It was my pleasure to oblige them with a ball-handling or shooting demonstration. With a teammate rebounding, I backed up to twenty feet and drilled in forty or fifty shots in a row. Everyone seemed to want to see this demonstration, and I got a bang out of doing it.

Dad and I experienced a fantasy year as we became household names in the world of sports, and the entire country monitored the progress of my mounting numbers, counting the days until the next collegiate record.

For most of the season, I was involved in a shoot-out with Niagara's Calvin Murphy for the national scoring title. I really didn't want to get caught up in the media attention pitting Calvin and me against one another, but every sports writer loves a good race. I managed to get in a groove going on scoring binges that helped me add to the totals. At the end of the race I finished with 1,138 points, 432 of which were field goals and the rest from the charity stripe. When the statisticians finished tallying the results, I ended the season with the best per-game average in the history of collegiate basketball—43.8 points. Murphy ended the year with a sensational 38.2.

My greatest number of points in one game came later in the year when the Tigers took on the Crimson Tide of Alabama. With the final seconds ticking off the clock, my teammate, Ralph Jukkola, stole the ball and unselfishly zipped a pass to me, screaming for me to shoot. I crossed the half court line and let it fly. The ball found its mark, and with that shot I broke Bob Pettit's Southeastern Conference single-game record ending the night with fifty-nine points.

At season's end I had set four national records, sixteen SEC records, and nine LSU records. I was voted the league's Most Valuable Player and placed on the all-SEC team. United Press International and Associated Press named me to their all-American teams. And the United States Basketball Coaches Association placed me, the only sophomore, on their all-American team with Wes Unseld, Elvin Hayes, Don May, and Lew Alcindor (Kareem Abdul-Jabbar).

Through all the fascination of the year, both my dad and I had to divorce ourselves from underlining the friction happening between us, the conflicts at home, and the trouble in the world in general. The late 1960s were explosive in many ways, and we tried to use basketball to provide a soothing escape from all our problems. Little did we know, the sport we loved could be blamed for many of the problems creeping in on us.

Dad had little time to concern himself with current events occupying the minds of most Americans. During the season, the North Koreans held eighty-three sailors hostage on the Navy ship, *Pueblo*. It made my Dad's blood boil to hear of the atrocity. The old Navy man in him wanted to captain his old bomber and retaliate. But, his mind was preoccupied with a battle of his own, and it wasn't on the court at LSU.

A special bond had developed between Dad and my sister, Diana; but unfortunately he couldn't give her a normal home life. Mom's illness worsened and the battle in the household began. It was up to Dad to single-handedly keep the family together, raise Diana, and do all the duties required for basic survival: cleaning, cooking, shopping. The load nearly crushed Dad.

Basketball had fed Dad and our family ever since Mom put her foot down and forced him to give up his thought of being an airline pilot. Ironically, basketball now became the wedge driven between Mom and Dad and me.

Mom had been faithful in her motherhood. She clothed us and fed us and was always there when we needed her. She made a concerted effort with Dad to infuse my life with the game Dad adored, and in so doing, she helped foster the worship I had for the game. For years Mom drove me to practices and games. She enjoyed sharing the excitement I experienced, especially when the records were broken and the media attention began in high school. She was so proud of me, and that pride could be seen throughout the house. Memorabilia from my career hung on nearly every wall.

But the thousands of hours of dedication to basketball had kept Dad and me away from the house and from her more often than not, and the loneliness became intolerable. When I became a celebrity in college I rarely shared the successes with her. The same could be said for Dad, due to the hours spent away from home building a winning program.

Unfortunately, Dad didn't see the true cause of Mom's decline in attitude and health. She successfully concealed a drinking habit, taking great pains in hiding all evidence from us. We knew she was ill, but never imagined the illness to be alcohol related. A beautiful woman was crumbling before our eyes, but we never realized she was inflicting the decline on herself.

Dad wanted desperately to bring LSU a winner, but with my mother sick and unable to care adequately for my little sister, Dad could not concentrate on the team. Despite the problems, LSU gained some respect across the country that year. Dad began looking like the coach Jim Corbett had promised the school. When LSU won ten of its first thirteen games that 1967–68 season our spirits lifted in spite of the depressing home situation. The pressure began to build, though, from the tremendous media attention we were receiving. One night the frustration reached a boiling point. We were tied with our opponent in the last few seconds of the contest and Dad called time out to huddle the team around him for a last-second play.

"Let's settle down and play like we know what we're doing out there," he shouted, as he scribbled a play on paper for the team to see. "We're going to run 'Big John,' " he said.

Big John was one of Dad's many special plays—this particular play tailored for the last five seconds in a game. The team listened intently as my dad reviewed the role of each man. As he explained, I hovered over him and started shaking my head. Finally I interrupted, "I don't like it Pop. It won't work."

In a split second, Dad stood to his feet and hit me on the head with his fist. Eleven thousand people watched, but it didn't matter to him.

"I'm the coach . . . you're the player!" he shouted. The other Tigers were stunned as they watched him disciplining me.

"You listen, and do what you're told!" he continued.

I stood in a shock, surprised he would do such a thing. We stared at each other for a moment, then he finished his instructions.

When we threw the ball inbounds, the synchronization of screens allowed me to be open for an uncontested ten-footer, just as my dad said I would be. I popped it in, and Big John made us the winner that night.

After the game I was cornered by newspaper men and local television crews. I fielded questions about the game, but made no comment on my dad's outburst. When the media left the locker room and arena, I met Dad in the corridor. It was a strange moment. I hadn't been physically disciplined since I was a kid, and it sure wasn't in front of several thousand people.

"Pop . . . ," I called out as he walked out of his office. He locked the door and turned to me. "I . . . I want to apologize for what I did."

"I shouldn't have whacked you like that," he said in an apologetic tone.

"No, no, . . . you were right. What I said . . . it was like tellin' you, you didn't know what you were doing out there," I answered. There was another strange pause as I looked at him. I noticed for the first time how the stress at home and on the court was taking its toll on him. His crew cut was greying, and his eyes were red and cloudy from the strain.

"I love you Pop." Dad needed to hear the words of encouragement. He looked up at me and smiled. The bond was as strong as ever as we walked down the empty hall together.

During the dark days of the roller coaster year, our family received some good news when Ronnie was discharged from the Marines. We were so happy that he was one of the fortunate ones to come home from Vietnam alive and physically whole. Dad figured with Ronnie back in the States, he would have one less thing to worry about. But, that didn't prove to be so. That night I borrowed Dad's car to pick Ronnie up at the airport and more trouble began.

Dad had a brand new Plymouth GTX. The Navy blue, two-door beauty with a spit-shine finish was Dad's pride and joy. When I asked to borrow it to pick up Ronnie, he squirmed a little, but gave in, knowing how much I liked the car and wanted to impress my big brother with it.

All was peaceful until Dad left for work the next morning. He walked out under the carport and found the remains of his GTX. Dad let out a scream of horror that could be heard for blocks.

"Helen! Helen!" he screamed to Mom as he burst in the back door of the house. Mom couldn't imagine what had happened.

Before she could ask, Dad continued, "Hold me back! I don't want to kill them!"

She grabbed him by the arms, "What's happened? What's wrong with you? Kill who?" she asked in a frightened voice.

"My boys!" he shouted as he stared out the window. "I just can't believe it. Look at my new car!" he moaned as he looked at the mangled front end and side. He couldn't believe what he saw. It had to be a bad dream!

After a moment, reality set in and the blood boiled. "On second thought, don't hold me back, I'm gonna strangle both of them," he threatened.

Though he wanted to inflict bodily harm on us, he didn't. We tried our best to explain how it was an innocent accident that could have happened to anyone. "We're lucky to be alive, Dad," we told him as we stated our case. In truth, we had partied, celebrating Ronnie's return, and I had carelessly wrecked the car.

The car incident was painful to Dad, but it wouldn't be the last trial with me off the basketball court. One night some friends and I got drunk in a local tavern and proceeded to destroy the men's restroom. The fiasco started as a show of strength among us. One of the LSU football players rammed his fist through the wall, then challenged me and one of my basketball buddies to follow suit. I took the challenge and ran my fist through the wall. After a few drunken cheers, my buddy rared back and jammed his fist into a stud in the wall. As he writhed in pain, the football player and I gave the wall a few more whacks. A couple of strong kicks later, the wall toppled. The wall was obviously temporary or just an incredibly cheap one, because we found ourselves staring at parked cars. The wall lay at our feet in the parking lot. When we stopped laughing, we went back into the bar as if nothing had happened.

The next day Dad got a call from the bar's proprietor. He threatened to go to the papers and to the law if his wall wasn't repaired immediately. Dad got on the phone and cursed me up one side and down the other, telling me to get the building materials and put the bar back together or forget about coming home.

After the wall was reconstructed Dad and I had a long talk. "You're a role model, now, Pete! Don't you know little kids are looking at you—watching everything you do?" Dad reprimanded.

"That's not my fault."

"The heck it isn't! You're in the eye of the public, and you've already lived your nine lives," he retaliated.

"I play basketball, Dad! It's supposed to be a game, isn't it," I replied. "This whole thing's like a business now. The fun has gone out of it!"

I vented some frustrations. Basketball wasn't the fun little game I had fallen in love with so many years before. Basketball was a job, and all the economics of the system demanded that we treat it as a profession and not just an enjoyable activity. As Dad and I looked around us we saw how everything, our entire livelihood, was based on the business of basketball. If it wasn't run like a business, it would fail. This reality was hard for us to face.

By the time summer rolled around, I needed something new to recharge my attitude toward the game. The opportunity came in an invitation to the summer all-star game to be held in Indiana.

Hoosier fans had heard of my exploits, but it would take my best effort to make an impression on them. The game was a prelude to the Olympic trials.

Though I played with two pulled muscles, and scored only sixteen points, my lowest in college competition, the game's officials saw fit to present me with the Star of Stars award for outstanding performance. For the first time in history the award was given to a sophomore. The honor certainly helped recharge my attitude.

My next outing was to Albuquerque for the United States Olympic trials.

The morning of the tryouts the headlines in the *Albuquerque Tribune* read, "Dazzling Maravich Heads All-Star Cast Tonight," a flattering headline. Despite my dad's warnings about the politicized selection of the Olympic team, I felt I had a good chance at making the team and at the very least wanted to try.

Dad's warnings proved to be prophetic, and I should have listened hard to him. We played three games, and I was on the court about two minutes per game. On the final day, I knew the Olympic selection committee had been denied the opportunity to see what I could do, so I decided to have some fun and display a few elements of Showtime. During the pregame warm-ups, I put on a performance for the few people who were in the stands. I shot behind-the-back lay-ups; half court hook shots; and ricochets from the floor. I did all my spinning tricks, then I began to dribble. I basically did an abbreviated Showtime clinic. But, that's all they would see of me. I didn't make the team that went to Mexico City.

During the sticky, hot Louisiana summer, Dad was confined to his duties at home with Mom and Diana. Though he was tied down, he wanted the clinics to continue so he sent Ronnie and me out on the road. I enjoyed the time with my big brother. We joked and laughed as we traveled together, and the old bond that had been missing since Vietnam started re-forming.

After the last clinic of the summer, I felt like celebrating and hitting some bars with Ronnie. That evening I pulled the car off the road and turned into the drive of a seedy tavern.

"How about a couple of beers?"

"Just one then I'm going back to the motel," Ronnie answered.

The response came as a surprise to me since Ronnie was usually the ring leader between us. "Suit yourself," I replied.

When Ronnie left with the car I slid into a booth and ordered another beer. As I sat there a girl sat down beside me and asked if she could join me. Before too many words were said I felt a poke on my shoulder that sent a pain shooting down my back. I turned angrily to see a huge bearded man, dressed in jeans and a T-shirt hovering over me. His piercing eyes were deep set within his obese face, and his breath nearly knocked me over.

I didn't want any trouble. I tried to politely reassure the guy that I had no designs on his girl. The moment was tense when the bartender spoke up.

"Take it outside," he said. "You fight in here, I call the law."

"Look, I don't want any trouble," I said, trying to prevent any further harm.

I just rolled my eyes wondering how something so stupid could happen so fast. I wanted to make a getaway before I ended up with a broken arm, or worse. The bartender, detecting my anxiousness, assisted by showing me the back door. I didn't think twice about the alternative route. I thanked the bartender and walked through the back of the tavern to the exit. I cringed as the old screen door squeaked on its rusted hinges as if announcing my departure.

I anticipated being jumped in the parking lot by a man twice my weight. In the dark I managed to see a board next to the trash cans. I picked it up to use as a weapon, then peeked around the corner of the building to see that the coast was clear. I spotted a phone booth at the corner of the lot. If I could make it to the booth, I could call Ronnie to come rescue me. After a few cautious steps, I walked briskly toward the booth. Suddenly, a man shouted obscenities at me. As I turned around he began to walk toward me. I had never run from a challenge before. As I stared at him I felt the blow of a blackjack graze the back of my head. Before I knew what happened they were both upon me. I started punching at not one, but two men. In seconds they beat me to the ground, and I lay nearly unconscious.

With blood running out of my nose and streaming from a cut above my left eye, I lay flat on my back trying to focus my eyes on the enemy. Suddenly, the girl from the bar kneeled down beside me and started laughing. Without warning, she pointed a handgun at my face and stuck the barrel to my mouth.

When I realized what was happening, it snapped me out of my grogginess. The girl laughed and said, "Pistol Pete—you're dead."

I began thinking of all the junk in my life, and how one pull of the trigger could make it all go away. I would suffer no more disappointments. I wouldn't have to try for the championship ring. I thought I would finally have peace if she would just pull the trigger. In my mind I could hear myself screaming, "Pull it! Pull it! Pull it!" But, she and her friends merely laughed and left me lying in my own blood.

After a few minutes, groggy and disoriented, I found myself in the phone booth trying to call Ronnie. Blood streamed down my face as I heard the sound of a car pulling up beside me. Seconds later I was in the car—a squad car, and I was booked for disturbing the peace.

The next morning Ronnie picked me up at the county jail. The police found out who I was, and they shuffled me out the back door to avoid reporters.

We walked down the back hallway. When we opened the back

117

door, we were bathed in the flashing lights of reporters' cameras.

For me the summer was over, but the personal battles weren't. Somehow, I knew the war between what the public perceived and what was really happening in my life would continue.

14

A New Love

The country was still mourning the assassinations of Dr. Martin Luther King, Senator Bobby Kennedy, and the deaths of hundreds more brave American soldiers in Southeast Asia, when the fall semester began at LSU. The year was 1968.

Football, as usual, occupied the minds of Louisiana sports fans when we returned to classes. Though my notoriety had reached a national level I tried to maintain some degree of normality to my everyday life, making friends and renewing friendships from the year before.

One evening, I entered my favorite bar in Baton Rouge before the place opened for evening business. The proprietor and I enjoyed some lively conversation, shared a few beers, and solved a few of the world's problems until the evening crowd came in.

A few hours later the place started hopping with students and locals showing up at the popular watering hole. As music from the juke box played rock 'n' roll, people gathered around as usual and the jokes and stories began. The place became filled with cigarette smoke, the smell of beer, and the laughter and conversation of people looking for a good time.

I found happiness in a place like that for a few hours, but the feeling was short-lived. The next morning always brought me back to reality as I woke with a hangover to face the turmoil of the day ahead. Regardless of the temporary good time, it was the only escape I enjoyed.

This night was no different. After several beers and dozens of my own jokes, I started feeling loose and uninhibited. I laughed and felt as though the party had just begun when all of a sudden I caught the image of a girl in the mirror behind the bar. The sight of

119

her sobered me a bit. I strained to see as people crossed behind me and periodically blocked my vision of her.

To my surprise I had spotted a beautiful girl I'd never seen on campus before. I grabbed the edge of the bar and did a 180 degree turn on the stool to get a direct look at her. As she spoke, I saw her laugh and push her long hair away from her face and onto her shoulder. I couldn't believe my eyes. In an instant I was totally infatuated with her.

I turned back on my stool and kept an eye on her in the mirror as the evening progressed. She was unaware that I was monitoring her every move. The physical attraction to the girl was amazing. I felt a burning desire within me unlike I had ever known. No one had ever caught my eye as she did.

A couple of days later I ran into the guy I had seen sitting with her that night. I asked who she was. "Her name's Jackie," he said.

I couldn't help myself. I was so taken with her, I blurted out, "Can you get me a date with her?"

He said he was willing to set me up on a blind date with Jackie. When she heard the news, her eyebrows raised in a questioning manner. "I don't go out on blind dates, and who's Pete Maravich anyway?" she asked.

"You're serious?" he asked in disbelief.

"Yes," Jackie answered.

"He's only the most famous college basketball player in America, that's all. I can't believe you've never heard of him," he replied.

"I don't follow sports," Jackie replied.

He did some quick thinking, and said, "But, Jackie, you have to go out with him. At least, do me a favor and see him one time. I already said you'd go out with him."

Jackie was never hurting for dates, so for her to accept a blind date with me was pretty unusual. To her, going on a blind date meant you were desperate.

Her image in the pub's mirror was etched in my mind, and I couldn't erase it. There was something inexplicable about the feelings I had for the mysterious girl.

The day of the date, I picked her up at her parents' house, then we went to a party before the Tiger football game. Everything was going well until I made the mistake of beginning to drink with my buddies.

By the time the game rolled around, I was a bit intoxicated and had a difficult time finding the tickets. Jackie helped me search. But we came up empty. With the second half of the game beginning, Jackie asked me to check my pockets once again. Sure enough, the tickets were on me the entire time. We managed to see most of the last quarter; at least Jackie saw most of the last quarter. I missed a lot of it because I was in the men's room.

To help smooth things over, we headed for another party. We pulled into the Catholic church driveway to park the car. I began to joke with her about the things that had happened that day, and everything I said seemed to make her laugh. Both of us sensed that despite our glaring differences of opinion and backgrounds, opposites were attracting; and we liked the feeling, though neither of us could bring ourselves to admit it that night.

We talked for a while longer and I sheepishly leaned over and kissed her. Suddenly, we were interrupted by a tap on the window. We were startled to see a priest standing beside us. Jackie immediately started telling him we were just talking. After a moment listening to her explanation, the priest merely asked us to move our car.

After our initial twelve-hour date, I got the feeling that it was either our last or the beginning of something special.

A few days passed, and I asked Jackie to go to a rock 'n' roll concert. I didn't know how to express my feelings to her about our first date. Strangely enough, Jackie had similar feelings about the night. She would later admit to me that she felt some things were said that shouldn't have been, but her feelings for me were very special.

Surprisingly, she turned me down for the concert telling me she was sick. I was smart enough to put two and two together and figured she didn't want to see me again. In reality she had a date for that night and didn't want me to think she was uninterested.

A few days passed and I received a phone call from Jackie. One thing led to another and we became steady partners my junior year. She provided a much needed balance in my life as the basketball

121

season started and dominated most of my time. I really needed some stability that year.

Her thoughts were with me during the Christmas holidays as we left Louisiana for the Oklahoma City All-College Tournament. The Tigers managed three major upsets. I led all scorers and won the MVP (Most Valued Player) award for the three-day affair. Dad's coaching helped us knock off unbeaten, nationally ranked Wyoming, the favored Oklahoma City University team, and ninth ranked Duquesne.

I broke another Frank Selvy record by scoring a record fifty-one field goals and thirty-six free throws for a total of 138 points for the three games. My teammates, including Jeff Tribbett, Rich Hickman, Dave Ramsden, Ralph Jukkola, and Danny Hester, turned in spectacular offensive and defensive performances to round out the scoring.

The tournament's highlight came in the final seconds of the Duquesne game. Duquesne boasted its own version of the twin towers when they brought to the tournament Garry and Barry Nelson—real twins. Near the end of the game, we picked away at a ten-point deficit. We took the lead and seven seconds later Duquesne went back up by one.

With fifteen seconds left on the clock, Danny Hester went to the line with a one-and-one situation and sank both baskets. Then, I got fouled and put the game on ice with two free throws.

When it was over, the nation's leading defensive team had been stunned. Coming into the game against LSU, Duquesne had only allowed fifty-two points per game. With the help of my teammates, I scored fifty-three—thirty-two coming in the second half.

We returned to Baton Rouge as heroes, gaining more national attention and a great deal of respect for ourselves as a team to be reckoned with in the 1968–69 season.

The praise picked up right where it had left off at the end of my record-breaking sophomore year. Jackie's complete disinterest with the game gave her a totally different outlook on the records and the fame. She thought it was silly for kids to go crazy over the guy she was dating. Basketball was just a game in her opinion, and she wasn't about to get caught up in the nonsense of who won and who lost, or who scored the most, or who fouled out. Those were things that a fanatic could deal with.

It didn't take long for me to realize that it was her attitude that helped me maintain my sanity through all the craziness of the season. Plenty of people in my life were telling me how great I was and how proud they were of me. Jackie became the honest voice in my life that brought me back to earth, win or lose.

The relationship struggled through some jealousy stages, mainly on my part; but our differences and jealousy became less and less important as the basketball season pressed down on both of us.

Our season began with an impressive 7–1 record giving southern Louisiana new reason to hope that LSU would be the team to take it all. Unfortunately, we ran into the SEC and things started to crumble. We had every conceivable kind of defense thrown at us. The majority, of course, were designed for one purpose in particular, and that was to stop me.

I could barely handle one loss, much less a dozen or more, so I was fortunate to have someone to help me during 1968–69. Jackie was there to get my mind off the business of basketball and on to other things. She saw that basketball made me miserable off and on the court when the team lost, and it didn't make sense to her. So, she purposely directed our conversations away from basketball-related subjects and focused on things we could both share.

Keeping my mind on other things sometimes helped relieve the physical pain I suffered as well. Some days Jackie would find me scratched and bruised up and down my arms from all the contact on the floor.

I had always been referred to as the kid with the pained look on his face, but by the middle of the season I had a legitimate reason for my expression. One game I scared Dad and me when I was undercut going in for a lay-up and my knee buckled as I collapsed to the floor. The team doctor and my dad wanted to take me out of the game, but they quickly realized I would leave only at gunpoint. Once I stood up I felt like I could finish the night. I scored another twenty-six points and ended the game with fifty-four. Dad was glad he let me stay in.

My mind was focused on one thing on the court; but off the

court, for the first time in my life, I had to find a balance between the game that meant everything and a person who meant a lot. Jackie had become very special in a short time, but basketball had a sixteen-year head start on her.

Besides Jackie entering my life, I savored several other personal highlights my junior year. I broke Bob Pettit's LSU career mark the night I passed 1,972 points. When LSU played Kentucky, I scored my 2,097th point, topping the two-season NCAA scoring record set by Elvin Hayes.

If the season had to be capsulized by one moment, it would be the shot that occurred in the final game of the 1968–69 season against Georgia. The clock was running down the final minute of the second overtime, and since we had the lead I had fun running out the clock by dribbling through the Georgia defenders. After a few seconds, the partial Georgia crowd were on their feet clapping for me.

With seven seconds left, I dribbled toward the corner of half court; and with three seconds to go, I let fly a hook shot and began walking toward the dressing room. The ball hit nothing but net. I was congratulated by the Georgia team and carried off the floor by the Georgia cheerleaders!

The game wasn't televised or filmed so there is no video record of the night. The length of my forty-five foot hook shot has grown through the years, making for better folklore. People still refer to it as "that hook shot."

What a great way to end the year! We really enjoyed playing hard for my dad. I broke my own point totals by scoring 1,148 points for the year, while shooting fewer shots. I shot .444 from the field and .746 from the free-throw line, and I also topped my assist record with 128. I knew Dad was proud as my name appeared on every all-American team in the country once again.

Through all the trophies, telegrams from government officials, fan letters, and gifts, one stable influence in my life kept my head out of the clouds—her name was Jackie. Her companionship provided me a refuge in which to lose myself, if only for brief periods of time. She didn't threaten my status or demand my time. Jackie was just the sensible slice of reality in a world thick with temporary accolades.

15

The Quest

The night was January 31, 1970, and the eyes of the sporting world focused on the old Cow Palace to see the most prestigious record of collegiate basketball fall. Everyone antici- pated my passing 2,973 points before the night was over. Ole Miss was to be the victim as they came to Baton Rouge on the cool winter evening. I needed 39 points to surpass the impressive record of Oscar Robertson.

At the half, we led the game 53–40, and I went into the locker room with twenty-five points. The Tiger fans had waited anxiously for this night; the night they could say they saw it happen. I just wanted to get it over. I was never concerned with personal records. Playing to the best of my God-given ability was my attitude and motivation.

As I headed for the door, Dad took me by the arm and said, "Keep your mind on the game."

He picked up his clipboard and noticed a cold cup of coffee sitting on a chair. He picked it up and tossed it in the trash. "Forty- two cups in one day. I'm killin' myself," he mumbled.

The John M. Parker Coliseum filled with applause and shouting when the Tigers returned to the floor for warm-ups. The half began as expected when we came out full throttle and began to bury our opponent.

With 7:50 left in the game, I brought the ball down the court and pulled up to hit a fifteen-footer. The shot tied Oscar Robertson's record 2,973 points. I was only one shot away, but the next three minutes seemed like forever. On the next four Tiger possessions the shot wasn't there or I failed to connect. The fans and I had taken just about all we could by the time I came down for my fifth attempt.

"One, one, one," the crowd shouted in unison as I dribbled down court. I launched myself from the hardwood floor twenty-three feet from the goal. High in the air, and almost fully extended, I flicked my wrist sending the ball up and through the hoop.

The court was immediately flooded with fans and the news media. Two of the Tigers, Bob Lang and Al Sanders, put me on their shoulders for the ovation from the standing-room-only crowd. I was given the game ball as the cameras flashed from every direction. The whole stadium was filled with cheering and applause, but the only reaction I could manage after the initial smiles and waves was pleading with my teammates to put me down so we could finish the game!

After order was restored, I ended the night with fifty-three points and twelve assists.

In the locker room, I tried to put into words my feelings about the night. "This is the greatest honor of my life," I said, as I squinted into the television camera lights, "Oscar Robertson is the greatest player ever, and I'm really fortunate to break his record."

"How would you describe the shot, Pistol?" a reporter shouted above the crowd.

"My favorite."

Photographer's flashes lit up the room as reporters crowded in for exclusive pictures and interviews. Dad was so proud he could have lit up the room all alone with his beaming countenance. Congratulatory hugs and handshakes were coming from every direction as friends and well-wishers shared in my dad's pride.

I was glad that I could help my father succeed in fulfilling Jim Corbett's prediction that Dad would bring respect to the LSU program and basketball excitement to the South. If Corbett had lived through our stay in Baton Rouge he could have seen firsthand some results of his decision making. Before Dad took over the basketball program, the school averaged fifty season ticket holders. During our years there, they sold the four thousand limit every year, far in advance. A new Assembly Center was planned that eventually became one of the finest basketball facilities in the country with seating for over fourteen thousand; freshman, varsity, and visitors' dressing rooms; coaches' offices; sports information offices; building administration offices; kitchen facilities; and much more.

Accolades from all over the country poured in, and letters and telegrams filled my apartment. One telegram read, "Dear Pete, You can take great pride in your recent efforts which have established you as the leading scorer in major college basketball history. I just want you to know the Nixons are among your fans saluting this success. Congratulations! With best wishes, Sincerely, Richard Nixon."

But, through all the glory and temporary gratification, I found myself slowly becoming a slave to the never-ending pressures placed upon me. The demands started coming in all forms and from every direction. I felt a constant expectation from everyone who watched. I knew I had to perform at a certain level or I would disappoint people. I also learned that a lot of the pressure I felt wasn't even in the realm of basketball, but in all the trappings and responsibilities surrounding me as a public figure.

When the Tigers won seven of eight games after Ole Miss, we were considered a legitimate threat in basketball circles. For the first time at LSU I could see the possibility of post-season play. But, my concentration was constantly divided in so many directions. I was involved in pregame interviews, post-game interviews, a television show, a radio interview. Things got so bad that I was even being interviewed when I went to the toilet. After games I might be the last to leave the locker room, only to walk into the hall where dozens waited for autographs. I managed a smile and signed every single one, sometimes taking an hour or two to finish.

As the tension mounted, I selfishly felt I was justified in going out and doing what I wanted to do off the court to escape from the world around me. Back then being a good role model wasn't a priority in my life, although I knew everyone in the public eye was considered a role model, and I was no different.

The public had a mixed perception of me. They seemed to either like me or hate me. When the Tigers visited other arenas, hecklers were on me with name-calling and throwing debris. One night it was so bad before the game, I turned to the crowd during warm-ups and tried to manipulate them. When they jeered, I looked up into the stands and threw a behind-the-back pass to one of the hecklers. I smiled and motioned for them to throw it back to me. When I got the ball back, I flipped another trick pass to another heckler. Before long, I had won over some of the spectators. When the game finally got started, the name-calling was hardly noticeable.

A similar thing happened to us at Oregon State. They made it known that they were going to take the air out of the ball or stall. Their plan was to hold the ball and shoot nothing but open lay-ups.

I was guarding Freddie Boyd, a lightning quick, play-making guard. He was in the corner of the court holding the ball, and I started saying, "Shoot the ball, Freddie, nobody wants to see this!"

He said, "I can't!"

"Drive for a lay-up!" I said.

"I can't!" he answered.

I was so frustrated, I sat down on the court and crossed my legs. Again, I replied, "Can you make a lay-up now?" He continued to hold the ball and I shouted to the fans, "Tell Freddie to shoot the ball."

After a moment, the fans began to boo. The booing became contagious until the entire arena was filled with their discontent. From then on, they quit their stall offense and played an "up tempo" game. Their plan worked, but they didn't anticipate me making thirty of thirty-one free throws to set an NCAA record.

I didn't expect everyone to like me; I wasn't that naive. But it got to me a bit when spectators deliberately showed up to heckle my family. That was my boiling point, and it was most obvious one night when we played at Alabama. I had twenty-two points in the first half, but the game was marred by a fight and the ejection of my teammate, Danny Hester. We were spitting nails because of the one-sided calls by the referees, or lack of calls. When Dad and I were both slapped with technical fouls, the place erupted with cheers and jeers from the Alabama fans who desperately longed to thwart their Southeastern Conference rivals. However, the heckling had a reverse effect on me; the more I heard, the more intensely I played.

When the final buzzer sounded, I had scored a record sixty-nine points in a 106–104 defeat. The frustration of the loss was devastating to us. To add insult to injury, as I walked off the court one heckler in particular didn't have the wisdom to stop. In a flash I was after him, wanting to tear him apart. My teammates followed, and threw some punches of their own.

The fight proved nothing, but it did underscore the turmoil Dad and I were suffering. Newspaper articles reflected the misunderstanding and public perception commonly held in sports circles regarding the incredible strain we were under, but no one outside the Maravich home knew the whole truth about what had really been transpiring for the last few seasons.

Early one night I went to my parents' home and found Mom sitting on the couch, half asleep. For several months she had complained of being too sick to do much of anything, and normally a rest on the couch would have been no surprise to me. But this particular night was different. As I looked at her, I noticed how she had changed physically. I realized then my preoccupation with the season and all the activities surrounding it had kept me from spending any time with my ill mother. Her decline took me by surprise.

Mom seemed to have aged overnight. Her hair was unkempt, and her clothes were wrinkled. Dark half-circles had grown under her eyes, and the lines in her face were deeper and more defined.

At first I didn't want to disturb her, but I looked around the house and noticed for the first time the extraordinary deterioration of the place. At one time Mom would have picked up the tiniest piece of lint off the rug; but as I stared at her hand, I watched the ashes from her cigarette drop into a little pile on the floor.

"Mom? What's goin' on?" I asked in a voice full of confusion and frustration.

Mom sat up, snapping out of her half-sleep. "Oh, hi, Pete. So, you decided to come home, huh?" she asked, as she forced herself to a standing position. I frowned and stared at her. This wasn't the mother I knew. Immediately, I sensed a behavior I had seen in myself.

"What are you doing to yourself?" My voice shook. "Look at you!"

She pushed the hair from her eyes and tried to act sober, but it was obvious her sickness was totally self-induced.

What followed was an argument very uncharacteristic of the mother-son relationship we had shared for over twenty years. I accused her of destroying herself and our family because of drinking. As I look back, it was the pot calling the kettle black.

She stood her ground and shouted that she had never been a part of my life. She claimed it had always been Dad and me and basketball, and she never fit in.

The words pierced my heart. She had been a part of our lives and just as persistent as Dad in luring me into the game. She had driven me to practices and gone to all my junior high and high school games. I couldn't believe she would say such a thing.

She continued her tirade telling me I had no idea of the loneliness she had suffered. I could not understand the pressures she had been through trying to hold the family together with the money problems, Ronnie in Vietnam, and raising little Diana. She raged on and on until I had taken all I could.

I was convinced alcohol was doing all the talking, but the hurt was still the same. She lifted her cigarette and I knocked it from her hand and grabbed her arms. Enraged, I shook her and screamed, "Why are you doing this to yourself, Mom?" I remember fighting back tears as I leaned her against the wall. She batted her eyes, lacking the strength to put up a fight.

I had never felt such a rage in me. My blood seemed to boil as I looked at a mere shell of the mother I loved. *It was so unfair*, I thought as I glared at her. She stood helpless, trying to act sober.

"How could you do something so stupid! How could you?!" I screamed as I fumbled for words to express my disappointment and anger. Suddenly, I doubled my fist and rared back. With all the strength I could muster I drove my fist past her head and into the plaster wall.

The act of violence scared Mom as well as me when I realized what the rage had made me do. I pulled my shaking hand from the hole in the wall and stared at her. In that tense moment I wanted to tell her how much I loved her. Without speaking, I turned and walked out of the house, leaving her alone.

Dad had told me of Mom's sickly condition, but it wasn't until I saw firsthand that I realized the severity of what was happening to her. To me it was as if the decline had happened overnight, though I knew my dad and Diana had been fending for themselves for a long time.

The pain ate at me, but to the outside world I maintained the image the public wanted to perceive. I put on my plastic smile and carried the hurt into the only refuge I knew, the basketball court. I vented my anger, frustration, and disappointments within the confines of the arena.

When I confronted Dad about what I had seen at home, he immediately scoffed at the idea. "Your mother is sickly, Pete. That's a terrible thing to say about her," he answered defensively.

"I tell you, Pop, she's hitting the bottle. She has to be," I replied, trying hard to be tactful, yet direct. "Check around the house if you don't believe me," I added, hoping he would investigate.

"I'll be wasting my time, Pete. I live in the same house with her, you know. Don't you think I'd smell something or find a bottle or something?" Dad replied, trying to defend his wife and himself.

"For her, Pop. You gotta check it out . . . promise me," I pleaded. He realized things had gone far enough. The last thing he wanted, however, was to admit the woman he loved was hooked on alcohol. It all seemed so unbelievable and cruel. If Mom was sick, Dad felt as though he'd be betraying her trust if he went snooping around the house looking for evidence. But, as he thought it over, he came to the conclusion that I was right. If she was drinking, he did owe it to her to find out and try to help her.

"Okay, I'll check around. Not that I think I'll find anything, you understand. I'll do it for you so you'll stop worrying about it," he answered.

The first opportunity he got, Dad casually began looking through the house for clues. He found no empty bottles in the trash, but then again, that would be too easy. He started looking behind the furniture and in the closets, but still nothing to incriminate Mom.

Dad felt guilty as the thoughts of betrayal filled his mind. But as he continued searching and didn't find anything, his guilt turned to reassurance that her sickness was truly a medical problem unrelated to a dependence on liquor.

For his own peace of mind, Dad kept searching. He couldn't wait to tell me my theory was unfounded, and the anger directed at my mother was uncalled for.

Unfortunately, the moment Dad was ready to pronounce Mom innocent, the first small bottle of liquor showed up in a cushion of the couch. Dad went numb as he stared at the flask.

"No . . . no, it can't be," Dad whispered aloud. All the things he had read about alcoholics began returning to his thoughts. He remembered they were the cleverest of all addicts, devising ways to hide their problem from family and friends. If Mom was a classic case, it wouldn't be easy to find the evidence.

Dad scanned the house, trying to assume the mind of my mom for a moment. He walked into their bedroom and searched the drawers and the clothes closet. He felt pockets and boxes, then began sticking his hand into pairs of shoes on the floor. Sure enough, he found another bottle in an old pair of shoes Mom hadn't worn in years.

The search continued, and with every discovery Dad's heart sank a little deeper. He fought back tears of anger and sadness as he found a tiny bottle in the chandelier. He shook his head in despair as he opened a vinegar bottle in the kitchen cabinet. Mom had replaced the contents with hard liquor.

After the search, Dad sat at the kitchen table wondering how he could have been so blind. But his blindness hadn't concealed the facts as much as Mom's cleverness. She had become a master illusionist, convincing Dad that she was truly ill. He was hurt to think she could pull such an act and get away with it.

A few days later, Dad worked up his nerve and confronted Mom. She admitted her habit, and after some discussion she made some promises. Eventually, the promises to quit were broken. Before long the situation was totally out of control and Dad found no help in correcting the situation. His time was consumed with trying to raise my little sister and create some kind of normal life for her. Dad had to continue as he had been, being breadwinner, babysitter, and father.

The Maravich family home soon became a place for sleeping only as far as Diana and Dad were concerned. The morning began with him fixing breakfast and taking Diana to school. At three o'clock

Dad left LSU to pick her up and take her back to the gymnasium where she would sit on the bleachers and read or do her homework until practice ended. From practice, they made their nightly stop at Bob's Big Boy restaurant for dinner.

Despite the tremendous external pressure on Dad, he led us to a 20–8 record and a post-season invitation to the National Invitational Tournament. We entered New York City on a wave of publicity. The Tigers were due for another major tournament showing, and we had a good ensemble. Rich Hickman and Jeff Tribbett had complemented the quick offense for four years. Al "Apple" Sanders and Bill "Fig" Newton brought some height and board strength to the team. And Dan Hester improved to average sixteen points a game and help us a lot with point production.

Though we had one of the highest team scoring averages, we were not the favorites of the tournament. Al McGuire, the coach of the Marquette Warriors, wasn't pleased with some of the goings on in the NCAA tournament, so he opted to send his team to the NIT. The Warriors were immediate favorites and rightly so with a 22–3 season.

Other formidable opponents were North Carolina, Georgetown, Duke, St. John's, Duquesne, Army, and Louisville. In the field of sixteen teams, none was a pushover and Dad quickly reminded us of that fact.

Playing in New York and Madison Square Garden was the highlight of my college basketball career. I had always liked New York basketball fans and admired their knowledge and love for the game. Dad had reminisced with me about the old days when the Big Apple was king, the hotbed of basketball talent.

Our first opportunity came against the Georgetown Hoyas, who applied the brakes to me as soon as I took the floor. The Georgetown defense was exceptional and for the first time in my career I was outscored by a teammate. I ended the night with only twenty points. I did manage to redeem myself a little bit at the end of regulation when I made two free throws with nine seconds left to ice the game at 83–82.

That kind of game was not what I would choose to win over anyone. When we entered the tournament I was holding twenty-five collegiate records, eleven of which were national. No one

133

would have guessed it by watching that game. I was first to point out to the media that I had played possibly my worst game ever, and I let them know I hoped to redeem myself against Oklahoma. Dad came to the same conclusion about how I had performed, and he left me with a warning that I'd better straighten up fast.

For our next game the Garden was full of New Yorkers come to see for themselves if all the national attention and articles filled with superlatives were fact or fiction. Even if the hype was all fact, it would take quite a performance to win over fans who had seen it all before. I tried hard, but fell short of what I knew I could do. We won the game, and advanced into the semi-finals against Marquette, the tournament favorites.

Again, I answered reporters' questions and again admitted to my horrible play. Dad agreed. Though I had scored thirty-seven points, we had made too many mistakes, and Dad knew Marquette would chew us up and spit us out if the same blunders occurred against them.

After fielding numerous questions and signing autographs, I dragged my worn body back to the hotel room. My legs were like rubber, and my body was bruised and scratched from the beating we had taken on the court. Fatigue was overcoming me quickly. I even canceled an appearance on the "Dick Cavett Show" in order to get to my room and close the door. I had had no peace and quiet since I stepped off the plane, and I needed it badly.

Unfortunately, back in the hotel room nothing changed. Despite telling the desk to hold all calls, the phone kept ringing off the hook. People were still looking for me: some were fans; some were writers and reporters. Regardless, I didn't want to see any of them.

Several of my friends came over. I locked the door, and we relaxed with a six-pack of beer. All I wanted to do was forget everything. As I leaned back on the pillows of my bed, I shared memories of the past four years with my buddies. We laughed and told stories of games and girls and stupid tricks we had pulled at LSU.

The party continued into the night and I got totally wasted. Sitting on the threshold of my very first championship, I drank to feel good and forget. I had finished a great four years of playing the game, and all I wanted was to celebrate the end of it all.

When morning broke, I could hardly keep my bloodshot eyes open. When the game time rolled around, I began to pay dearly for my foolishness. Kind reporters blamed the sluggish performance on my past two outings when I ran full tilt as the play maker. Those who knew saw me still reeling from a poorly timed hangover.

The real victim in the fiasco was my dad. He had taken the team so far, and he watched his dream of an NIT championship fade before his eyes. He could not coach his way out of it. No trick plays could've salvaged the finale.

Marquette showed no mercy. They played an excellent game and crushed us, 101–79. I struggled to score a pitiful twenty points. The night was very embarrassing to us all. But I don't know how anyone could have felt worse than I. Because of my foolishness my college career ended without fanfare.

When the realization of what had happened finally sank in, I was totally devastated. My stupidity not only contributed to a loss, but humiliated my dad, and that was unbearable. I couldn't even look him in the face. I could not tell Dad the truth about the all-night party. The trip back to Louisiana was long and quiet.

I ended my college career averaging 44.5 points per game and scoring 3,667 points in three years. But no championship.

BOOK FOUR

TWO DOWN, ONE TO GO

— 16 —

Millionaire

"Cocky? That's a guy who thinks he's good, but isn't."
The reporter probably had a feeling the entire interview would go that way. I was eluding most questions being fired at me, and when I did answer I avoided any hint as to what professional team I would choose.

In the summer of 1970 some were making bets as to how high the bidding would go. Team owners saw the packed houses on the collegiate level all through the southern states when the Tigers played, and they figured my name on their roster might do the same for their professional franchise.

In the beginning of the seventies, professional sports entered the world of high finance. Because of increased television coverage and the commercialization of pro sports, the number of television viewers and fan support were phenomenal. As a result players began reaping the monetary benefits.

I now had a price on my head because I drew crowds and helped pay the bills; and since the name of the game was bigger profits and not amateur sports, the accountants and business managers smelled dollars to be made.

I was climbing the ladder of a dream set in place years before. The scholarship was behind me; it was time to get the million-dollar contract and win the ring.

My dad sensed the fury beginning to brew in the professional ranks. The high rollers in the Pistol Pete sweepstakes were squaring off, and he could hear the calculators pecking out numbers neither of us had ever been close to.

Low pay and struggling was the norm for Dad all his life, and he wanted life to be different for me if he had anything to do with it.

Dad knew firsthand what financial insecurity could do to a guy, and he didn't want that heritage passed down to his son.

As far back as I could remember, Dad and Mom scraped to get by. Dad was really hurt when he heard people making statements about how he and I must be raking in the big bucks at LSU. One coach even remarked to the public that the university had pampered us and kept me comfortable in a new Cadillac for four years. In reality, I drove my old Volkswagen each year at LSU.

As for Dad, he had signed his five-year deal at fifteen thousand dollars a year, failing to incorporate a raise or cost of living increase. Coaching had never panned out financially for him, so he wanted more than ever for me to succeed where he had fallen short.

The major players in the contest for my services were the Atlanta Hawks of the NBA (National Basketball Association) and the Carolina Cougars of the younger ABA (American Basketball Association). Atlanta had made a trade earlier with San Francisco and as a result had acquired the Warriors' first-round pick in the draft. When the selection began, no one expected the Hawks to have a shot at me since Atlanta was third in line to announce their choice. But Detroit opted for Bob Lanier and San Diego took Rudy Tomjanovich—both teams filling specific weaknesses in their respective line-ups. The Atlanta Hawks then selected me.

The stage was set for a shoot-out as the NBA franchise placed their offer on the table across from the ABA franchise. The Cougars' owner was ready to deal heavy to land me.

As usual I went to Dad for advice. Dad hired a lawyer friend to handle the negotiations. He wisely told me to relax and let things develop.

Things heated up, and the offers got richer and richer. The Carolina franchise was going full throttle. The Cougars scheduled a meeting in New York City with their lawyers and my counsel, wanting to discuss the final loose ends of a multimillion dollar deal and sign the papers on the spot if both parties could come to terms.

Ironically, I was broke and couldn't afford airfare to fly to the Big Apple to sign a multimillion dollar deal! Dad came to my rescue and scraped together airfare and a little spending money for both of us. I was so thankful to have him in my corner giving me advice and helping calm my nerves. As we flew to New York we discussed our options and thought them over quietly.

"I'm gonna be rich, Pop. Is this unbelievable?" I whispered leaning back in the comfortable airplane seat.

"Don't get too excited, yet, Pete. We'll listen to what they offer, then we'll go from there," he replied.

I detected an unsure tone in his voice. "You don't want me to sign with the Cougars, do you?" I asked.

He sighed and leveled with me. "I'm not ruling anything out, Pete. It's just I've heard the rumors about the ABA merging with the NBA, and I'm afraid you could get burned and lose some money in the deal," he said.

"Is that all you're worried about?" I asked, sensing the distress in his voice.

Dad looked me in the eye. "You've always wanted to play against players like Jerry West and Oscar Robertson. You won't find them in the ABA," he said, then paused for my reaction. I was silent. "The NBA has that thirty-year pension plan going. You have to look down the road," he continued.

"Let's see what the Cougars give us first, then we'll decide," I replied, wanting to stay on a positive note.

When we arrived in New York, we went to a nice midtown hotel and met our lawyer and the lawyers from the Carolina team in a room reserved for the negotiations. The discussions began; the Carolina team had come to play hard ball. There were restaurant franchises, cars, lots of money, and a movie contract.

The negotiations dragged on into the night and eventually into the early morning hours. When Dad took me into the hall for a breath of fresh air and privacy, he almost had to anchor me to the floor. I was so excited by the offers I was ready to sign then and there! In my mind I had most of the money spent already. I pictured my new cars and imagined owning all those restaurants, and of course I wondered how soon we could begin shooting my first movie. As Dad tried to restrain me, my lawyer Art came out into the hall and dampened my spirits.

"What do you think, Art?" Dad asked.

Art moved away from the door to make sure he wasn't overheard. We followed, eager to hear his reaction to it all. "I think they're phonies," Art said.

"Naw, are you serious?" I asked, not wanting to believe it.

Art was very serious. His advice was to leave and set up a time for another meeting in a week. Dad swallowed hard, knowing he didn't have the money for another trip, but he wanted to play by Art's rules. After a short conference back in the room, the lawyers agreed on a plan to resume talks the following week.

The lawyers packed their briefcases and left the room. Art followed suit and left Dad and me alone in the room to think about what had transpired. After more discussion, Dad suggested we get some use out of the room for the night. A little after 5:00 a.m. we climbed into the double beds, bushed from the lengthy negotiations.

After a couple hours of trying to sleep, we were up and on our way to catch our 9:00 a.m. flight. As we rode the elevator to the lobby Dad told me of his restless sleep. He didn't have a good feeling about the way things had gone. I still wanted to keep a positive attitude.

We walked through the lobby, discussing all the fabulous aspects to the offer. I was so pumped up about it all, knowing I would sign the most lucrative deal any athlete had ever known if we agreed to their terms. Dad listened patiently as we walked to the front door.

As we started outside to get a cab, we heard a voice coming from the reservation desk. "Sirs! Sirs!" the man called, as he waved an ink pen in the air. Dad turned back to notice the man was calling us. I just shrugged to Dad, as we both wondered what was happening. When we walked back to the front desk we got some surprising news.

"You are checking out?" the man asked politely.

"That's right," Dad answered with a curious look on his face.

The man jotted a note on the guest register as he said, "That's fine. And how will you be paying?"

"Paying? No, no, the room was paid for by the fellows from the ABA," Dad smiled, finding the mistake humorous.

"I'm sorry, sir, but no one paid," the man said.

We couldn't believe our ears. If ever we needed a sign as to which offer to take, this was it. Dad had eighty-two dollars on him and the room for the night came to eighty-one dollars, including tax. Dad was furious and embarrassed as he shelled out nearly every dollar on him.

After the room was paid for, we walked out to the curb to hail a cab. Dad had one dollar on him and I had a ten dollar bill. Our stomachs were growling for breakfast, but we were far from the airport and needed all our money for cab fare.

We arrived at the airport, and I paid the cabbie with my ten dollar bill. Dad pulled out his single and handed it to the driver as a tip. The driver sarcastically said, "Oh, thanks very much."

His attitude burned my dad. Dad threw open the front door on the cab and leaned in. "Hey, if you don't want the buck, I'll take it back!" Dad growled.

The cabbie left with the dollar. Dad and I went back home to prepare to sign the deal with the Atlanta Hawks.

It was a proud day for us, the day of the news conference in Atlanta. Photographers' cameras flashed as I held up my new Hawks jersey. Lou Hudson was wearing number 23, Ronnie's number; so I chose my college scoring average and had number 44 emblazoned upon the uniform.

For a few days I was in the Guinness book of world records as having signed the largest contract ever agreed upon in the history of sports. I had become a millionaire. And, to add gravy to the pile of money, the team threw in a Plymouth GTX, a place to live in Atlanta, and a country club membership.

The thousands of hours finally paid off, literally. I had worked and dreamed of it actually happening. Though some people marveled at the million dollar figure, I quickly informed them at the press conference that by 1980, players would be making over two million dollars for a single year. Again, like that reporter who interviewed me when I was twelve, they laughed.

17

Like A Hawk

Young people were still bucking the system in 1970. Hippies and Yippies through the sixties represented the most vocal counterculture crying for change. As Americans entered the "me decade," the call for peace and love was beginning to blend into "do your own thing."

I traveled the country telling young children to do their own thing, but not in a rebellious spirit. I put another twelve thousand to fourteen thousand miles on my Volkswagen bug driving from one clinic to another preaching the gospel of basketball; spreading the positive message of what the game can mean in the life of a youngster.

I fervently believed that an athlete, or any young person in general, should have his long-range goals in life planned by the eighth or ninth grade. Though few children considered the next month in advance, I constantly challenged the students in my basketball clinics to start making plans for their futures and stop wasting time.

The attitude of planning ahead was so natural to me, that I found it frustrating at times when I stared into the empty eyes of listless teen-agers. I detected their lack of motivation and focus.

"You're wasting your lives if you don't settle down and work, work, work," I told them. "You will never become a great basketball player if you fail to dedicate yourself 100 percent to perfecting your game or if you fail to practice."

At my camp in Pennsylvania, a local teen-ager and his gang entered the gym looking for one of my campers who had messed with one of their bikes. They came ready to bust some heads. After some coaxing and a firm threat, I convinced the young man to put away his knife and talk with me. Two hours later I saw a change in his attitude. I encouraged him to get his life cleaned up and focused on something constructive. It was a man-to-man talk the likes of which he had probably never heard. I got the distinct feeling no one had ever taken the time to sit and listen to the young man's problems and situation, then offer him any advice on how to deal with them.

To my satisfaction he sought me out a year later to tell me of the fantastic progress he had made in his life. He had a good job, had gone back to school, and was planning to go to college. That day I realized the life-changing effect I could have on a young person's life through the camps and clinics.

My message fell upon hundreds of ears the summer before I entered the world of professional basketball. My speech carried much more weight than ever before with the young students since I was speaking from practical experience.

I painted a picture of satisfaction beyond a child's wildest dreams. The future could be bright for the young boys or girls who applied themselves to completion of their highest goal.

This time in my life was quite uplifting. I thought I had the world by the tail as I traveled about anticipating the beginning of rookie camp with the Atlanta Hawks.

Meanwhile back in Baton Rouge, Mom's alcoholism began having a direct effect on Dad's ability to do his job as a coach. Since the late 1940s, when he first wrote his book on scouting, Dad had perfected his skills of spotting great talent. But since Mom's illness, his movements were restricted.

Dad wanted desperately to comb the country for exceptional talent and bring a national championship to LSU. When he scheduled time to search out talented big men and lure them to Baton Rouge, domestic troubles seemed to flare.

One weekend Dad took a chance on leaving town, sensing a lull in Mom's radical behavior. With much trepidation he left Diana with Mom, but ever cautious, he called my five-year-old sister constantly from Tennessee to check on her. All was well in the beginning, and Dad proceeded with some recruiting duties. When he returned to his hotel room the first night, the phone rang and to his surprise when he answered he heard Diana crying. Things had taken a turn for the worse at home. Dad could only grip the receiver as he listened to her cries. Diana explained between her sobs that Mom was breaking every dish in the house, and Diana had sneaked to the telephone. Her voice shook as she pleaded for her daddy to come home. My dad had never felt more helpless in his life. He told her to run to her room and lock the door. She wasn't to open it until he got home.

It almost killed Dad to hang up the phone. He envisioned the worst happening to his baby. He hung up the phone and asked God to protect her.

He seemed to have few options at the time. He considered hiring a private plane, but he didn't have the money. Then he calmed himself and waited patiently for his flight home. That was the last time he tried to personally recruit for LSU. The limitations placed on him by Mom's illness haunted him during his entire tenure at Louisiana State.

When I arrived in Atlanta I moved into my two-bedroom town-house with little fanfare. The modest dwelling was comfortable and quaint, unlike the swank abode one would expect a rich, young rookie to occupy. My only frills were the new billiard table and monogrammed towels and wash cloths with the name *Pistol* emblazoned on them.

My transportation was upgraded several notches, however, as I relinquished the faithful Beetle and climbed behind the wheel of my new Plymouth GTX. I was ready to arrive at rookie camp in style.

The first day of camp, the place was active with reporters and Atlanta brass hoping to catch a glimpse of why they had spent so much money getting me. When I arrived, I felt the spotlight shining brightly on me, and I knew the sharks were ready to strike if I didn't pan out and prove myself to be the showman and the player of the year the college ranks had labeled me to be.

I discovered it wasn't just the critics who were waiting for my downfall; other rookies in the camp had arrived to try to make the team, and what better way to do so than to make me look bad. The scrimmages included hopefuls such as John Vallely, Herb White, Bob Christian, and Bob Riley.

Once the ball was in play, I knew the Atlanta Hawks' coaches and administration would have their eyes on me, and I didn't want them to be disappointed. I don't think they were. Despite a weak ankle from a recent sprain, the camp was a great success for me. I could see smiles everywhere—or almost everywhere. A few of the Atlanta veterans wandered in to check me out and the reaction was skeptical to say the least. They were doubtful as to whether my style would gel with the Hawks' ensemble of the year before.

The skepticism was just the beginning of ego trouble found so often in the world of sports. Atlanta was coming off a terrific year that saw them win the Western Division, and every player from the championship team was returning for another shot at the crown. For me to get adequate playing time, someone was going to have to ride the bench for a while. Economics alone would pressure head coach Richie Guerin to start me.

The rumbling started subtly. A rumor circulated that the rookies as well as the veterans would be out to work me over on the court and make me earn my salary the hard way. I still wasn't full of bulk, and a few good blows could do considerable damage. But the threats never evolved, leading some to believe that team officials wanted me protected, apparently spreading the word that abusing the new acquisition was unpardonable.

Ironically, the dollar figure of my historical contract was not only protecting me but also stirring the hot coals of dissension in the ranks of the veteran players. An untested rookie receiving more money than anyone in the league had everyone talking, and the effect on the Atlanta players was predictable. After all they were the ones who had worked hard and struggled to the playoffs. The closer the season came, the louder the grumbling became. One of the Hawks starters refused to sign his contract, protesting the big dollars given me. His request was for one dollar more than I was paid or they could kiss his services goodbye.

The action began to cast a shadow upon the cohesiveness of the team. I didn't want to get caught up in a contest of who's greatest among us. I realized my salary was public knowledge and could be taken as a slap in the face to some of my new teammates, but the inequity wasn't my fault and I could not do a thing about it. Still the grumbling continued and other players began to complain of the preferential treatment given to the stranger in town.

145

Caught in the middle was my new coach. Richie Guerin was an ex-player, and he knew firsthand the importance of harmony on a ball club. It was imperative for him to walk the tightrope between his talent and the front office. The struggle for Guerin was increasingly difficult the more my name and face were spread around in preseason. Adding insult to injury, the publicity specialists agreed the tag for our 1970 squad would be "The New Hawks," implying that the old Hawks weren't acceptable, and also implying that the Pistol was the shot in the arm they needed.

Like it or not, the veterans couldn't deny the new interest generated in Atlanta. People who had never attended a Hawks game before were buying tickets in advance.

The exhibition season began, and the discontent manifested itself noticeably on the court. When I got into the game I found myself in a foreign land, all alone. My style of play, which was a trademark at LSU, was incompatible with the rest of the team. Just as I felt I was finding my rhythm, the other four Hawks were awkwardly out of sync with me. My passes ended up in the stands, and on one occasion the intended receiver was hit in the head.

When I drove down the court and got double teamed, I found no help in sight. It was as if the team was letting me dig the hole in which I might bury myself.

The season began and the conflicts were still unresolved. The Hawks didn't match the demand of a dollar more than the Pistol, so they lost one of their consistent starters. However, this didn't mean that an automatic position opened for me. It was just the opposite. Richie Guerin wasn't convinced that I could cut it yet as a professional play maker, and he refused to put me in the line-up.

To my dismay the season opener found me warming a seat on the bench. The media and the new fans were vocal about the leading scorer in college history on the bench watching the game instead of helping it as they had hoped.

In the second quarter of the opener, Guerin gave me my introduction to a legitimate professional game. Before long I stole a pass, drove down the court, and shot a ten-footer for my first pro basket.

That season ABC decided to televise NBA games, and it was no coincidence two of their first three games featured the Atlanta

Hawks. Roone Arledge, the president of ABC Sports, was fully aware of the national interest surrounding my record-breaking college days; but he also appreciated the show business style I displayed on the court. The network hoped it would all add up to a decent showing in the ratings.

The constant attention from the press and television media just added fuel to the controversial fire. When the team's high scorer was interviewed after a game, he was asked questions about me. Even while riding the bench, I was often the focus of attention for the news cameras, and it only served to foster more resentment toward me. When the Hawks were on the road traveling to a game, I was doing public appearances or filming a commercial. When the rest of the team was being ignored, I was being interviewed for national magazines and newspapers. The bitterness continued, and the isolation grew. After weeks of trying I was ready to give up on winning friendships. I couldn't seem to make it work, and it didn't seem worth the trouble and effort.

Meanwhile, back on the court, Coach Guerin stuck to his guns and didn't rush me into the starting five. Not until the thirteenth game of the season did Guerin feel he had waited long enough to give me my first start.

When the night came, the change that came over me was remarkable. Beginning in the eighth grade I had started every game I ever played; but since being with Atlanta, I had to enter the game already in progress and was expected to be great coming off the bench stone cold.

If there was a remedy for sluggish performances, starting a game seemed to be just what the doctor would have ordered for me. I began to score like the front office wanted me to. Three games in a row I scored over thirty points and faith was restored in my abilities. This was the Maravich people wanted to see.

The Hawks marched into Madison Square Garden, and I sensed the opportunity to redeem myself from the embarrassment of the final NIT game the season before. I had disappointed my father, myself, and the New York fans whom I admired so much for their basketball savvy. As a Hawk I was facing one of the greatest teams in the country, the New York Knicks. My assignment was to go head-to-head with Walt "Clyde" Frazier. I was up to the challenge and ready to repay the audience for the show I had denied them in college. I scored forty points in a losing cause.

Unfortunately, my play was still in stark contrast to what the Atlanta club had been used to, and the criticism started again. As the club continued to lose games, the fingers kept pointing at Pistol Pete. The media criticism got so bad that I refused interviews.

But, for every critic on my back I could find two fans longing to see a new style of basketball. Like Joe Namath, I was attempting to put life into a sport that had become dry and boring at times.

"I'm just trying to push the game to its limits. We have so much to discover in basketball. Ten years from now, a lot of guys will be doing what I do. . . . Every team will have a seven-foot guy on their roster. Basketball has to grow and change if we expect people to keep coming and paying good money," I told reporters.

Slowly, but surely, my teammates and I played better together. They didn't totally believe in what I did on the court, but they started working with me a bit, helping me out when I got in a jam rather than letting me struggle and lose the ball. The results were noticeable as the turnovers decreased and the Hawks started looking like a team.

Even Coach Guerin was a confirmed believer considering me the favorite for Rookie of the Year honors if I continued in my ways. I managed to shoot fewer times, but score more points. I tried to help control the offense and work for total team rhythm.

By season's end, my shooting percentage was better than it had ever been in college. I had a .458 shooting percentage, and averaged 23.2 points per game. From the free-throw line I shot 80 percent. At the end of the year I ranked eighth in the NBA in scoring with 1,880 points.

When votes for Rookie of the Year were counted, however, my name was third on the list.

We did manage to squeak into the playoffs, but lost the series 3–2 against the Knicks. I took it all personally as usual, but looked back on the turbulent season as a success. The world hadn't converted to Showtime during the season, but that didn't bother me. I felt as though I had taken one step closer to the championship ring, and it would soon be in my grasp.

I found some consolation at the end of my tumultuous rookie

year when I was selected to the most heralded all-rookie team the NBA had assembled. My teammates were Dave Cowens, Bob Lanier, Calvin Murphy, and Geoff Petrie. Though a championship ring was still a hope for the future, being grouped with the best of the newcomers gave me some sense of the belonging I was searching for.

In 1971–72 my season got off to a poor start, beginning some of the darkest years of my life. The personal reasons for that I'll share in detail in the next chapter of this book. Regardless of the poor start in 1971, I was pleased later in the season to receive news that my name was placed on the second team all-star roster with Rick Barry, Walt Frazier, Dave Cowans, and Elvin Hayes.

The next year, my third in the pros, I hid myself in my refuge of basketball and tried to forget all the rejection, criticism, and failure that had crept into my life. My retreat into the game eventually won me more acclaim as I ended the year with a 26.1 average and nearly seven assists per game. The players voted me a starter in the all-star game and cast their votes for me as one of the premier ten on the all-NBA team.

When the 1973–74 season began, *Sports Illustrated* magazine featured me on the cover and explained the reasons for Atlanta's first-place ranking after the first twelve games of the season. I was flying high again, scoring almost at will. The scoring tandem of Lou Hudson and Pistol Pete was expected to carry the Hawks through the year and hopefully into the playoffs. Unfortunately for all of us, we fell short and the results of the year changed my life.

18

Lost Loves

The years in Atlanta can only be described as a very dark time for me—a time of searching, a time of trying to be the best basketball player I could in a confusing and turbulent situation. I have never revealed the personal events surrounding those years and in doing so I share the innermost depths of my heart.

I was a self-proclaimed, self-made loner. As the isolation grew between the Hawks and me, a solitary life became even more the norm. All my life I had tried to find satisfaction from other people and gain acceptance, but after years of searching for approval the energy to do so began wearing me down.

When the spotlights were on me during my rookie year, the happiness was fleeting. I realized that to be accepted in the pros I would have to blend into the system to become a part of it. As a result I found myself on a collision course between what I was and what the basketball establishment wanted me to be. My style of play wasn't the style I needed to win friends and fit into the league. In fact when Atlanta played Philadelphia, the conflict was very apparent as a huge banner was unfurled that read, "Pistol Pete, why do hot dogs cost 2 million in Atlanta and 35 cents in Philly?"

Off the court, no comaraderie was developing. The barriers were large, and they became even larger as I foolishly tried to buy my teammates' friendship, offering to buy their meals for them whenever we went out to eat. For me it was truly a gesture of friendship. Just a few months earlier I couldn't even pay my cab fare. But to the other players it was a reminder of who had the bucks and who didn't.

The estrangement led me to find new havens in which to lose myself. I looked for things to fill my life with some satisfaction and happiness, because I surely wasn't finding either one playing basketball. I got into martial arts and studied karate very seriously during the summer months for the next few years, earning a brown belt. Karate paved my way into looking for inner peace through yoga, transcendental meditation, and eventually into some re- search of Eastern religions. Quite frankly, I needed something to fill the tremendous void in my life.

In the beginning of my second season I contracted mono- nucleosis. Before long, I dropped in weight from 205 pounds to a flaccid 168. The sickness left me so exhausted that I had to have help climbing the stairs of my Atlanta townhouse. Naturally, I never regained my true form that year with my continual lack of energy. Doctors had even told me that I was foolish to come back to play as quickly as I did, because of the seriousness of the illness.

Back in Baton Rouge, what was later to become known as the "Maravich Era" was coming to an end. Home life for Dad and Diana was still dictated by the ill health of my mom, and it took its toll on Dad and his effectiveness as a coach at LSU. He was con- fined to the capital city, and though he continued to attempt miracles with players recruited secondhand, the Tiger fans clam- ored for a winning team.

The stress that he felt was incredible. His 1971–72 season was a dismal 10–16 and Dad knew that his job was on the line because of it. But no one, including myself, could really comprehend the frustration he was constantly feeling. Coaching had been my Dad's entire life and winning was the only thing that would keep his job. Yet for the first time in his life he found himself in a no-win situation. He refused to reveal to the public his turmoil at home, thus resulting in LSU opting for a new coach, someone who could breathe life into what appeared to be a dying program.

For years I must admit that we both harbored a grudge against LSU. How could they have fired my father? I just couldn't accept the way the situation was handled. But in retrospect, how were they to know? How was anyone to know the true reason for Dad's inability to develop a winning tradition as he had done at NC State and other colleges?

Being fired for the first time couldn't have come at a worse moment in his life. The last thing he needed with his unstable home life was to be out of a job. In an effort to keep food on the table and maintain some self-esteem, he went straight to the phone and started calling friends to seek another opening. In a profession where jobs are as fleeting and difficult as the game itself, finding work wasn't easy. He realized that fact when he resigned himself to take the first opening he could find. With the job secured, he called me to inform me of what had transpired and to tell me about his new job at Appalachian State.

I couldn't believe my ears! Here was one of the most creative minds in the basketball world leaving major college basketball for the first job opening that came along. I pleaded with him to not be hasty in his decision. I wanted him to be more patient and to wait to find a spot with a major university, or to look for openings on the horizon in pro basketball. But he was hurt, concerned about his family's well-being, and wanted into a new situation as quickly as possible. None of my pleading could change his mind. Dad packed up the house in bitterness and left for his new job.

By the time I entered my third year with the Hawks, Dad, Mom, and Diana were settled in the mountains of North Carolina. Being the eternal optimist, Dad entered the new program with the gusto for which he was famous. But as soon as he ran his new players through a scrimmage he was instantly sick to his stomach. He had little or no talent from which to choose and a skeleton budget. Things were so bad that sometimes the team drove in their own cars to away games—a far cry from the atmosphere of major college basketball. The bleak season only proved to make the long winter nights in the frozen mountains all the more horrible. Dad's chances of recruiting were made even more impossible by the isolated mountainous location, a several-hour trip from the nearest airport. My instincts regarding his hasty decision proved to be accurate.

Dad was miserable, Diana was miserable, and Mom was slipping deeper and deeper into an alcoholic depression despite profession-al help. We all thought that after six weeks of treatment at Duke Mom would be all right. But the positive effects were short-lived.

Back in Atlanta, I tried hard to keep my mind off the family trials and to focus my attention instead on helping the Hawks to the playoffs. Little did I know how the trials would continue to mount.

Midway through the season the Hawks made a road trip to play the New York Knicks. The weather was nasty as we arrived in the Big Apple, and I remember vividly the rain and the blast of cold air that hit my face as I stepped off the bus at our hotel. About fifteen minutes later I felt a strange tingling sensation in the right side of my face. I noticed in a mirror that my right eyelid wouldn't close, and I began to feel a numbness. I didn't know what was happening to me. I urgently sought a doctor for some answers, and to my shock I was diagnosed as having Bell's palsy, an affliction that paralyzes half the face.

The doctor told me I would have to tape my eye shut to sleep. I wondered what else could possibly go wrong. His prognosis was of no consolation. "We don't know what causes this type of paralysis," the doctor explained. "It's been a mystery to us for a long time. Unfortunately, a cure for it is also a mystery." The doctor had little more to say. I could tell the physician was as bewildered as I, but I had to have concrete answers. I felt my immediate future was hanging in the balance.

"How long will I be like this, Doc?" I asked, nervously.

"I'm not sure," the doctor replied.

The paralysis had gripped the side of my mouth, and the words slurred out awkwardly. I felt like a stumbling drunk. "I have to know," I demanded.

"A couple of weeks . . . a couple of years," the doctor answered quietly, knowing the shock he was inflicting on me.

Despite the doctor's warnings, that same night I tried to play in the game against the Knicks. He had cautioned me and described the danger of someone sticking a finger in my eye, possibly blinding me. But I had to try anyway. However, because I was unable to close my eye, the air hit it constantly and caused it to burn so badly that I had to stop playing.

All I could think about was spending the next few years of my life suffering with this condition. What a pitiful end to a career I had dedicated my whole life to. Out of desperation, I found some big goggles that wrapped around my face and decided to wear them during the games. People laughed at me, but I figured it was better than sitting on the bench waiting for the paralysis to go away.

After thirty-two days with the palsy, it finally subsided. The dream was still intact.

Just as things started looking up for me, I received a telephone call from my brother, Ronnie. His voice on the other end of the line was as somber as I had ever heard it. He said, "Pete, Mom is in critical condition with a self-inflicted gunshot wound to the head." I was stunned. My first thoughts were, *I can't believe it; it can't be happening!* But with Ronnie's continued silence on the phone, the reality began to sink in.

Nothing in my life up to that point had ever caused the deep-seated emptiness I felt at that moment. I told Ronnie I was on my way to the airport, and that I would call him in forty-five minutes or so. I hung up, hurriedly packed some overnight things, and headed to the airport to take the first plane available to Charlotte, North Carolina.

Driving to the airport, my thoughts were, *Why? Why, Mom? Why would you do it; why would you do this to us?* My mother meant so much to me, and all of a sudden she was one heartbeat away from death. I pleaded with God, even though I didn't know Him or even care about Him until this moment of tragedy struck. "Please, God," I cried out, "Save my mom. Don't let her die, please!" I was begging with every breath, but I felt my prayers were falling on deaf ears. I even tried to strike a deal, to bargain with God, promising anything and everything if he would only spare my mother's life.

When I arrived at the airport, I called Ronnie, hoping that he would have miraculously good news that Mom was going to make it. With each telephone ring, my stomach ached more and more. I remember fans walking by waving and greeting me, but I couldn't acknowledge them because my mind was focused completely on my mother's situation. Finally, Ronnie answered and said very slowly, "Pete, Mom didn't make it. She's dead."

I will never forget those words because never had words left me so numb, so speechless. In that brief moment, my entire life with my mother flashed in front of me. I began to visualize what she was like when I was seven years old. I remember the day she encouraged me to shoot baskets with Dad out in the backyard. That day she helped launch my basketball career. I remembered all the years and the special moments like the day I told her Jackie and I were planning our marriage. Her face was all aglow. How beautiful, compassionate, and caring she was! But suddenly times like those would never be again. I knew that the demon of alcohol, which had gained a strong hold on her life, was the trigger that had led my mom to the horrible, senseless tragedy. Even though Dad had sought help from everywhere: clinics, hospitals, psychiatrists, nothing was able to break the incredible bondage that had gripped her.

I was shattered like a broken picture window. I knew I would never again be able to hold her, hug her, or even say, "I love you, Mom." I wanted frantically to do something—to scream, to punch someone or something. But nothing could erase the guilt and loneliness I felt. All those years I thought basketball was the cure-all for everything in my life. But that night I learned it couldn't cure anything.

After it was too late, I realized I had selfishly grown apart from Mom over the years. All that the world offered me, plus my own selfish ambition and desires, had become the first priority in my life, and my love and concern for Mom took a back seat to it all. My entire value system was twisted. And my basketball fame and all the external success that I enjoyed for almost eight years had finally taken its toll.

I always expected Mom to be there for me. Ironically, because of my selfishness and foolishness, I wasn't able to see her pleas for love. It took years for my mother to deteriorate. I couldn't believe how I had let the years pass by without seeing what would be the end result. In my ignorance and indifference, I assumed that the help my dad had gotten for her would eventually alleviate the problem; but it had only aggravated it.

I felt tremendous compassion and remorse for my dad, who had been struggling to be the breadwinner, as well as trying to raise Diana almost entirely by himself from the time she was two years old. He was under incredible physical and mental stress because of Mom's condition. But he, too, was helpless in knowing what to do. As I sat in the airport I pictured my family mourning our loss. I wanted so much to get there to hold Dad, to love him and to do the same with Diana. I wondered how she must be coping having seen what Mother did. I just wanted to hold her.

Late that night I finally caught a plane. I sat next to the window and leaned my head against it, gazing at the brightest star I could see, wishing it was all just a bad dream. The plane ride gave me more opportunities to reflect on my relationship with Mom. No matter how well-intentioned I thought my love for her, the hideous reality of it all was the meaningless, valueless priorities within me that had helped push her to the end of her life.

The plane touched down and I rushed off to rent a car to make the two and a half hour drive to Boone, North Carolina. It was very late, around 1:30 a.m. I had been on the road about thirty minutes when I noticed in my rear view mirror the flashing bright lights of a tractor-trailer rig. The truck seemed to be coming up behind me very fast. My speedometer registered about 50 m.p.h., and because of the single-lane mountainous road and the fact I was totally numb and completely stressed out, I didn't feel safe driving any faster.

Before I knew it, my rear view mirror was ablaze with high-beam lights and the sound of a blasting horn was ringing in my ears. He was a foot from my bumper! I became scared because there was no place to pull off the road or to let him go around, so I decided to try and lose him. I accelerated to 60, 65, 70, then 75 m.p.h.; but he was still on my tail, blinding me with his high beams and blasting his horn continually. I finally put the pedal to the floor and cruised close to 90 m.p.h. He finally started losing ground in his pursuit of me.

Suddenly, in the darkness I came upon a four-way stoplight that seemed to be in the middle of nowhere. I pulled off the road and hid the car behind a closed gas station. About a minute later, the truck pulled up to the light and stopped. Strangely enough, the truck stayed at the intersection for almost ten minutes. I just knew for some bizarre reason he was trying to figure out which way I had turned. I sat quietly hoping he wouldn't go the way I was heading. Finally, he made a left turn and I continued straight. With my nerves frayed, I wondered if there were any more surprises left for me that horrible night.

Eventually, I arrived at my parents' house where Dad came out to meet me. We spoke no words; we just shared a loving embrace, trying for a moment to erase the devastation of our loss. We went inside and stayed up the rest of the night, weeping and talking, trying to figure out what had happened. Dad told me when he had left the house that night, Mom was sober. While he was gone she consumed almost two fifths of whiskey that she had hidden in the house. She had become deliriously drunk. I know and believe with all my heart that my mom was past the point of controlling her own actions. Her will had finally been broken.

The intense pain and anguish we felt that night were terrible. I knew with time they would ease, but of course never be forgotten. My regret was that I had not shown Mom the kind of love and compassion that was now actively being expressed in our family because of her death. If only I'd shown her the same love while she was alive.

19

The Louisiana Purchase

One Saturday morning in the spring of 1974, a member of the Atlanta Hawks management called, and I was surprised when he asked to come over to my house for a talk. The call aroused my suspicions because management never really talked to players about anything.

When he arrived he immediately announced that the Hawks wanted to trade me. Of course this news was a blow to me. Any athlete suffers a blow to his ego when he discovers his club is no longer in need of his services and he's being traded. But in all honesty, I knew something was up with management by some of the trades that had already taken place; and the news wasn't that shocking. What made the situation unique was the fact I had a no trade clause in my contract.

The representative didn't let that get in the way. He told me of a new franchise called the New Orleans Jazz and all the positive things in store for me. He didn't really go into any details regarding their negotiations but instead talked about how I would be going home to play and how it would be a fresh start for my career.

At the time I wasn't too thrilled with the scenario he described. I enjoyed living in Atlanta and didn't particularly want to leave. Some people might wonder why I didn't just say no, since I did have that contractual right; but the realities of the game were different in the early seventies because players didn't have the options they have today. If I had refused the trade, I probably would have sat on the bench, collecting splinters. Facing the hard facts, I knew it was over for me in Atlanta—I had worn out my welcome. And what I thought about Atlanta's doings had no bearing on the situation.

The thing that really burned me that morning was the reply I got when I told him I needed time to be alone to ponder the news. He said, "I just have one other thing I want to ask of you. I have the two owners of the Jazz waiting in my car. They'd like to meet you."

That was the icing on the cake. It really angered me that they not only had the gall to come over and hit me with the news of a trade— but to have the new owners sitting in the car, knowing I wouldn't have any time to digest the matter was unbelievable!

Soon I resigned myself to the fact that what happened to me was all part of the big business of professional sports. Because of economics and the whims of others, players would be deserted at one time or another in their career, despite their performance on the court. To that point in my career I had witnessed other mishandled trades, but for the first time I realized firsthand what a cold, flesh-pedaling business basketball could be.

When you're in the game, you always hear of players being traded, but you never think of its impact until it's you. Almost everyone is traded once unless they are on championship teams. When your team loses, management feels they have to do something to get the fans back in the stands.

I didn't really have any close friends in Atlanta when I got the news, and I had no family to talk to since Dad and Diana had pulled up stakes and gone to coach in Sweden after Mom's death. I did share my thoughts with Jackie, and I felt better knowing she would be thrilled about my return to Louisiana.

But the rejection was tough to accept because being traded is another way of saying you're fired, and it really bruises the ego. I can't deny the bitterness I felt toward those who shunned me in Atlanta. When I left Georgia I couldn't help thinking of the people who had stabbed me in the back. But today I can look back and see that because of my own personal instability and rebellious nature I was no doubt my own worst enemy.

I was hurt and angry at the Hawks, and the only thought that was giving me any satisfaction was basketball revenge. My plan was to beat Atlanta into the ground every time we played them in the future, just as Moses Malone recently did after Philadelphia traded him against his wishes. He wreaked havoc on the Sixers and other teams in the league, and that was my plan for Atlanta after my trade.

To rub salt in the wound, Atlanta felt they had a real coup d'etat with the terms of the trade; terms I was unaware of until the papers came out with what they called "The Louisiana Purchase." Basically a team was being traded for one player as the Jazz traded its number one picks in the 1974 and 1975 drafts; its second picks in the 1975 and 1976 drafts; its second and third selections in the expansion draft; and Atlanta was given the option to swap first-round picks in the 1976 and 1977 drafts.

After hearing the details of the trade I knew it would be a long time before the Jazz could be a contender and my dream for a championship ring seemed to be slipping away. I also saw the volatile situation that I would be stepping into, because all the so-called external pressures would be on me. The Jazz management told me not to worry about it because they would back me all the way, but I sensed what was said privately didn't always take place publicly. In other words, it was easy for them to say they'd help; but I knew bearing the responsibility would fall on my shoulders. Editorials in the New Orleans paper read, "How can they trade so much for Pistol Pete? Is he really that good?" No one knew or understood I had nothing to do or to say about the details of the agreement.

The Jazz ownership seemed to be pleased with the trade. They had no doubt I could turn on a crowd and fill an auditorium, and apparently that's what the new franchise banked on. The Jazz management also believed my name could conjure up memories of the basketball renaissance the state experienced while I played at LSU. Although they traded any chance for a winning season, they must have felt it was a small price to pay for the cornerstone of their franchise. In the minds and pocketbooks of the Jazz owners, their gamble paid off. Crowds were lined up at the ticket window of the old Municipal Auditorium to witness the birth of the New Orleans Jazz. I viewed the trade as a major obstacle in my career, instead of seeing it as the opportunity I consider it today.

I remember clearly when I first dribbled onto the floor and heard

160

the screaming fans. I began to feel a certain air of optimism. However, optimism fades quickly when you lose.

As the season progressed, a shot at the championship was obviously light years away as we found ourselves firmly planted in the league's cellar. But the move back home did provide other benefits not found on the court. After coaching in Sweden for a year, Dad came back to the States to work as a scout for the Jazz. Then I truly realized how greatly I had missed the opportunity to share my innermost feelings with him.

Another reunion, or rather, union, happened in Louisiana when I married Jackie. She had waited a long time for me to settle down from my bachelor ways; and after all my searching, I knew I could never find anyone so dedicated to me. She was still the balance in my life, never overwhelmed by the fame, money, and career problems. She loved me and was devoted to me.

Oddly enough, even after our marriage the playboy image still followed me across the country. The truth of the matter was the media had created most of the image in college, and my followers drew conclusions on their own.

Newspapers referred to Jackie as the mysterious girl I never talked about. The mystique was a result of insisting my personal life remain out of the papers and letting the public make their own judgments about what went on off the court.

Getting my personal life in order was of primary importance to me as the months and years wore on. The vision of the diamond championship ring on my finger still existed, but it was a pale image of what it had formerly been. Basketball was becoming less of an obsession, and surrendering my every hour to the game had long since been abandoned.

For thirteen years I had taken losing games as a personal punishment, brooding over a loss as though it were the championship that kept avoiding me. I lived, breathed, ate, slept, dreamed, drank, and prayed basketball. Over the years the pressure I chose to place on myself, combined with my undisciplined lifestyle, took its toll.

I remember the year we played the Los Angeles Lakers during their winning streak. No NBA team in history had won so many games in a row, but for some reason I knew and believed beyond a shadow of a doubt that we would break their string. I was so pumped up about the game that I couldn't sleep; and like so many nights in my past, I needed a sleeping pill to help me doze off. The night of the game my adrenaline was flowing so much I started consuming too much mental and physical energy before the game started.

I walked into the Lakers locker room a few hours before the game. To my surprise, I saw Jerry West sleeping on a bench in the back of the room. I couldn't believe it! Here he was in the middle of keeping a winning streak going and he was sound asleep. He woke, and I asked him how he could possibly relax at a time like that. Jerry told me how he had learned that if he didn't totally escape from the game, his performance over the long haul really suffered. It was one thing in college playing thirty games, but a grueling NBA schedule consisting of over one hundred games would naturally wear one down.

That night the reality of his advice hit me as the Lakers destroyed us. I personally had one of my worst games of the season, feeling as though I were standing still trying to catch a speeding locomotive.

From that point on I did anything possible to avoid thinking of basketball outside the game situation. I started reading anything and everything I could get my hands on to fill my time, and all the searching led me into different fads. Since I had no contentment, and little happiness in life, I needed to find ways to escape from the reality of my circumstances.

"UFO-ology" was one of the fads I got into to escape. I read every thing I could get my hands on about UFO's, astronomy, and astrology, which led me into the fringes of the occult. I was intrigued with the possibility of life on other planets, and I remember thinking how nice it would be if creatures from another planet would come and take me away from it all. I know how off the wall I must have sounded, but I was looking for something to give me the inner peace I couldn't find within myself. Fortunately like many other fads, the UFO stage passed away.

In retrospect I would have to say the Louisiana Purchase was in the best interests of the franchise as well as myself. By the end of the 1975–76 season we found ourselves ahead of the Atlanta Hawks in the standings and no one could have been more pleased than I. I got some personal satisfaction and a feeling of retribution, but more importantly it was the first time in my life in which I started having some semblance of a normal life happening off the court. Even the bitterness started to ease. Best of all, the steadiness of my home life settled me to a degree and helped me regain a positive attitude that in turn helped restore my faith in the possibility of playing on a team that would win that championship ring.

BOOK FIVE

SHATTERED DREAMS

---------- **20** ----------

The Scoring Championship

The Jazz paid their dues as the Superdome in New Orleans was under construction. Games were first played in the old Municipal Auditorium, then we moved to Loyola Field House where the floor was almost four feet off the ground and a net was fashioned around the court to catch a player in case he had the misfortune of going out of control while diving for a loose ball. I likened the floor to the beginnings of the sport when basketball organizers literally wrapped chicken wire around the court to keep the ball in play. Players felt as though they were caged—hence the nickname *cagers*. That's just how I felt as the Jazz took the floor surrounded by its protective netting.

The intimacy we felt in the small gym was lost immediately, however, when we moved into our new home, the New Orleans Superdome. The massive structure was high-tech at its finest, and it served the needs of the New Orleans Saints football team just fine. But when a basketball court was set up, thousands of ragin' cajuns were needed to generate the feeling of a decent crowd.

What reservations I might have had about the lack of crowd support were squelched in a hurry. New Orleans fans were hungry for any kind of championship team in town, and they displayed their eagerness as they streamed through the gates to see us play. They loved having a professional basketball team in the league and very quickly, coming to our games became the thing to do.

A great testimony to the fans of New Orleans was the night the city was deluged with nearly a foot of rain. Streets were flooded and businesses shut down as New Orleans was crippled by the flood. Despite the weather conditions, fans still came in droves to support us. Hopes for a great season were running high, and we wanted to give it our best shot for them.

We could hardly believe the game was still scheduled as Jackie and I watched the water rising on our lawn, but playing that night suddenly became a reality as the Jazz called saying they would send the sheriff's department with an all-terrain vehicle or a helicopter to get us.

I told them we'd try to get there; and after a cautious drive to the highway, we were on our way to the Superdome where over thirty-nine thousand rain-soaked fanatics watched the Jazz bring in a new season of hope.

After the opening tip-off that night, I played on the talent and dedication I had established over the years. Like many of the previous years in the pros, I normally spent very little time in preseason conditioning. My off-season discipline and commitment had been virtually nonexistent. I was ignorant that as I grew older the abuse to my body from bad eating habits, alcohol, and an undisciplined lifestyle would have a destructive effect on me.

Ever since I was a little eighth grader I found myself constantly having to overcome sickness or injury to play basketball. Even in the pros I had had to overcome mononucleosis and Bell's palsy. I could never figure out why I was always getting sick, but I did know that my health was definitely standing in the way of reaching my full potential. I didn't see anything wrong with the way I ate because I was like most Americans who loved to eat a juicy steak or grab a hamburger and fries on the run.

Eventually, I decided to take the advice of a fellow player (from a previous team) who was into natural foods. He seemed to never be sick and always went the whole season without injury. On his recommendation, my new diet consisted of fruits, vegetables, fish, and some chicken. I had red meat maybe once or twice that year, but for the most part I stuck to a natural food diet free from salt and sugar. I couldn't believe how great I gradually began to feel. My new diet combined with lifting weights gave me energy that I had never known.

As great as I was feeling, I decided to not say anything about the way I ate to avoid being grouped with other so-called natural food eaters. Several players in the league were self-proclaimed vegetarians, but they cleverly concealed the fact that drugs and alcohol were still an important part of their regimen. When their performance fell off, management and the media quickly pointed to their diet as the problem.

In contrast to my first four years in the pros, I now picked up in the beginning of the season and was able to play full throttle. When I scored thirty and forty points a game, I received little negative press. The headlines spoke of my exploits and continued painting me as the most colorful and prolific of scorers.

With each loss the media, the fans, the team, and I needed something or someone to blame. This need to place blame only added to the pressure I was already placing on myself. After every loss I dragged myself back to the hotel room or drove myself home carrying the guilt of the loss on my shoulders. No matter how hard I tried I could only think of ways I could have won the game if only I had tried harder, or had more patience, or made all the easy shots I'd missed.

As more losses mounted, the media started writing about dissension on the team as the reason. The rumors continued and grew. Since I was leading the league in scoring and we still lost, I became the focal point of the blame. Some said our problems were caused from my shooting so much. But, basketball consists of individual players assuming a role on the team, and the coach must go with the talent he has. I remember when Paul Silas went to Boston that he assumed a defensive role on the team. He didn't care much about shooting; because Boston had shooters, they needed a defensive specialist and rebounder. When a basketball team is made up of players who assume their roles and they are good at it, whether it's shooting, play making, rebounding, or defense, the team will be a winner. This assuming of roles is especially true with weaker teams. It just so happened that the Jazz needed me to score for us to win consistently.

I remember one night I was so frustrated with all the junk that was said about me, I decided to hardly shoot at all. By half time we were leading by twelve, but I had only shot four times. When I walked off the court the fans were wanting some Showtime, so they began to boo. Coach Elgin Baylor grabbed me and said, "What do you think you're doing out there?" I told him I was just playing to win. He looked at me and said, "Then you need to be shooting the ball."

Between the demands I placed on myself and the external demands placed on me to perform every night, the pressure was unbelievable. But, this is the type of pressure that any highly visible player will receive. I read recently where Michael Jordan scored fifty-eight points and pulled himself out of the game with three minutes remaining. When asked why, he replied, "I already broke the team's scoring record, that was enough. If I had scored sixty, then the fans would have wanted to see sixty-three. It's just never enough, and there's a lot more to the game than that."

Ten years ago I faced the same dilemma. During one game against the Houston Rockets, I went into the locker room with thirty-five points at the half and I thought of quitting the game. I was tired of scoring and having to manufacture points night after night. I no longer desired to carry the burden. Michael Jordan is probably facing some of the same pressures each game as the league's leading scorer.

If I didn't manage to score over thirty points, with eight or ten assists and a few steals, I felt as though the night had been a total loss. This attitude grew until I considered myself a failure if I didn't reproduce the most fantastic night in my career every time we took the floor. Steadily, basketball became my own worst enemy. What once was my god and provider became the thorn in my side, and I couldn't help but become disillusioned. From age seven I had thought basketball could do it all for me; but with the pressure to produce eating away at me, I questioned why I was even playing the game.

Ironically, through all the soul searching, I was in the middle of the best year of my professional career. On February 25, 1977, we played the New York Knicks, a team I always enjoyed playing because of all the New York fans who'd be watching. Everything from the opening tip-off seemed to work for me. I couldn't miss as I drove down the court and pulled up for twenty-footers. With every swish of the net the crowd grew louder and seemed to move closer, giving me a feeling that is hard to describe. As the fans roared their approval, I kept pushing harder. When the game ended I had scored a record-setting sixty-eight points. At the time, only two other players in NBA history had scored more points in a single game. The media wrote that I had finally reached the level everyone had predicted when I came out of college and signed the big contract.

As morning rolled around the next day, I wanted nothing more than to stay in bed and hope the world would somehow disappear. All I could think of were the expectations of the New Orleans fans, the club owners, the coach, the players, my dad, and worst of all, myself. Something in me was still demanding that I surpass anything I had ever done. I figured the only way I would continue to be accepted by the public would be to score sixty-eight points again and again.

The 1976–77 season ended with my name atop the list of scorers in the NBA. I finished with a 31.1-point scoring average, but still we didn't even have a shot at the playoffs. That season was a banner year according to the record books; but without a shot at the championship, I found no fulfillment on the court.

Through all the burdens and triumphs of the year the bright spots for me came only at home. Jackie was a constant support to me, especially during the home stands. When the losing really got to me, she tolerated nights when I invited over a buddy or my brother, Ronnie, to spend all hours of the night drinking beer and escaping from reality. I knew deep down it bothered Jackie. She hated the times when I was under the influence of alcohol, but my mind craved the departure from the external pressures. I knew in my heart there had to be more. Basketball had always been my provider, but it wasn't providing me happiness.

21

Diary

Most of my attempts at personally recording feelings and events have been futile and short-lived. When I did manage to write a few thoughts in a journal, they consistently reflected my inner search for happiness and meaning in life. If I was depressed enough or in a very introspective mood I penned my thoughts, hoping they would somehow give me new direction and hope.

Recently, I uncovered a diary I started during the 1977–78 season with the Jazz. As I read it, I recalled that all my weighty thoughts in those days led me to enter my feelings in the journal for safekeeping. The journal began with a denouncement of my past, labeling it as a total waste, selfishly lived, and worthless. By that year I had come to realize that my external circumstances totally dictated my life and that it was easy to be happy when you're rich and famous, because you have so many things to distract you from looking at yourself in the mirror.

In December 1977, for some reason I took a good look at myself. I'm not exactly sure why, and to be quite honest, I don't even remember the content of many of the entries. But they obviously reflect the struggles that were happening within me, and they reveal the battles I was experiencing on the basketball court at that time:

December 30, 1977
I have certainly been rambling on, but I pray that before I'm thru with this entire life of mine, I will be happy, peaceful, and my mind at ease about life and God. How can I be unhappy? It is very simple. There are millions of people who have not found a deep sense of purpose and meaning. I am one of them. . . . With all the trophies, awards, money, and fame, I am not at peace with myself.

170

January 1, 1978

It happens to be the new year. Often I wonder if this will be the year of some great happening. Of course this always seems to be on my mind. Today was like most days, relatively boring. . . . Talked to Pop. His advice and conversation are one of the highlights of my days and life. He is such a kind, tender man, with compassion pouring out of him. He is the greatest man I know on this earth. I pray to God he lives a long and healthy life. He has meant everything to me. Jackie has been her usual funny self. She has such a glowing radiance. I hope my love for her will always be the same. Only growing.

January 2, 1978

The blame of this team's failure will continue to be on me, but I guess I must accept it and continue to play my game.

January 12, 1978

Losing ruins all our road trips. But, somehow I must be patient. Keep my head, although the abuse shall really start now. If I were a fan, I would scream and demand this and that also.

The years of playing had taken their toll on me and it became apparent at the beginning of the 1977 schedule that I was ready to take a rest. In one entry I wrote that I must somehow find the "energy and enthusiasm to get through the rest of my career." Only one thing kept me playing harder than ever: hoping for a shot at the playoffs. I knew it was the key to the championship ring; and if I didn't play all out, the team wouldn't make it.

The season progressed, and I had a decent year despite our won-loss record. But physical ailments began taking their toll:

January 8, 1978

I am a physical wreck. My knees are hurting very badly, I guess I have patella tendonitis. But, I continue to play. I really am down now. I cannot play to my physical capabilities and it really hurts me. . . . I've got to learn how to cope better with losing. Every game that is lost I think I could have won!

Entries in the journal read like a sports update regarding the Jazz. I wrote of internal conflicts and even rumors of trading me to get the team out of a rut. Talk circulated suggesting the Jazz would never be winners or make the playoffs as long as I was on the team.

171

When word got back to me, I was angry. The rumors seemed to be exactly what I needed to fire me up and prove that management's opinion was dead wrong. Through the worst physical pain yet, I continued to contribute and help the Jazz get onto the winning track and into playoff contention. Our success angered those who hoped for my demise, as we compiled a streak of wins. Though we were winning, I became more reflective and philosophical about the whole thing, trying to rationalize why I had never played on a championship team.

January 22, 1978
   I feel God will never let me have what I desire. I wish I were as dedicated to the Lord as I once was to basketball. Really, whatever happens will happen. I have had a great career. I have been very fortunate. I have to walk with my head up.

My worries of a trade subsided as we positioned ourselves closer and closer to the playoffs. At the beginning of our most important winning streak, my excitement grew as I wrote: "I hope the Lord lets me win only in one place—on the floor. I have to keep playing well."

Anxiety and anticipation were in the air as the Jazz showed actual improvement and signs of creeping into a playoff berth. The winning streak was intact, and I managed to overcome the deterioration and pain of my ailing knees.

   Again I found myself hoping for miracles to open the way to a championship ring as I wrote:

Janaury 24, 1978
   Fantastic win! Our sixth straight. If the Lord could just let us keep winning it would solve everything. But, we have a nine-game road trip in February. We would have to win four of the nine to have a chance at the playoffs.

The media was having a field day. I was in a groove and we were playing like a legitimate contender for the Central Division crown. As I had hoped the fans hung with us and supported our efforts. One entry in the journal reads, "The crowd was with me. They chanted, 'Pistol!'"

The city of New Orleans was behind their team as the glimmer of hope peeked over the horizon. Could the young franchise really make it into post-season play? As the streak rolled on, I entered:

January 29, 1978
Unbelievable! We won our eighth straight game. We have really snowballed. I had a great game—35 pts., 11 assists, and 5 steals. Boy, does this feel great!

The ninth victim for the Jazz streak was scheduled to be Buffalo. I was charged and ready to help sustain the team's drive, and never was it more apparent than in the third quarter of the contest. The reality of winning nine straight hit the whole team, but no one on the squad was more elated than I, and I let it be known on the court. Knowing we had more than a good chance to get in the playoffs and start our run for championship rings was an incredible feeling. With time ticking away, I rode the crest of the crowd's enthusiasm. They were with us. They were with me. Everything we did filled the arena with waves of applause and shouts of approval.

With a comfortable lead, and the game assured, I rebounded a missed shot and faked an overhead pass. I started dribbling, then saw Aaron James breaking down the side of the court. One of the Braves players tried to stop my forward progress on the fast break, so I faked left, jumped in the air and threw the ball between my legs some forty feet down the court over the outstretched arms of the defender. The crowd went wild when Aaron grabbed the ball in full stride and slammed it through for two.

What no one seemed to notice was I had fallen to the floor writhing in pain. As the elation died and the crowd came to its senses, a pall fell on the arena. Something had snapped in my knee and the pain was excruciating.

My next entry in the diary reflected my fear of facing the reality of the situation:

January 31, 1978
I got hurt tonight. When I hit the floor in pain, I felt my career was over. It was intense pain for over a minute. I thought I had ripped my tendons up, especially when I heard the popping noise. . . . I have a badly sprained knee. I feel fortunate not being hurt worse. My career could have ended on that play. I hope to be ready by the Cleveland game. After 49 games I am first in scoring, sixth in assists, eighth in

steals, and fifth in free-throw percentage. This has been my best year to date. I hope I heal quickly and we make the playoffs.

At first the doctors gave me promising news. They thought the damage was limited and told me I'd be back helping the Jazz into the playoffs in no time. They couldn't have been more wrong. I tried to tape it up and play, but there was something very wrong, and the swelling and pain were constantly present to remind me of that fact. After more examination, the doctors came up with a different analysis of my situation. They had to break the solemn news to me—news I wasn't prepared to hear. The damage was too severe for any hopeful prognosis. I would have to have an operation.

To make matters worse, the Jazz won only one more game before our winning streak ended. The only glimmer of hope was the fact that we would have to lose twenty of thirty games to blow our chance at the playoffs. My name was on the disabled list and as I watched from the sidelines in my street clothes, the Jazz racked up eight straight losses. All of a sudden, the media claimed the team couldn't win without Pistol Pete in the line-up. They had come full circle from the days when they suggested I should be traded, exemplifying the fickle approach the media has to the game of basketball. All I could do was sit miserably and watch from a distance:

February 13, 1978
For the first time, I feel my career may be over. I drove across the bridge to think things out. I spent about two hours over there watching the waves break against the wall. One thing I do not want is to play on a bum leg the rest of my career. It would hurt me too much. My insides would turn knowing I could not do the things on the court I've always done.

Once again I had let my outward circumstances affect my inner peace. All the searching, all the changes I promised myself in my diary seemed of little importance. As the days wore on I even quit bothering to pen my thoughts. I couldn't face the fact that all the odds were against me regarding my knee's recovery, and the depression reflected itself in my rehabilitation. The knee would never be able to stand the punishment of the moves I was used to doing. They were too jerky and quick to continue on a damaged knee.

In a time when I longed for stability my life, my job became as unstable as my legs. But I refused to let my dreams of a championship ring be dashed. As the Jazz continued to lose, I worked harder than I ever had to get back in the line-up. I think my first game back was against Atlanta, an appropriate opponent for my comeback. I pitifully hobbled around the court for four quarters, scoring seventeen points in another losing battle.

All I could think of was hopefully getting on a winning streak and the momentum possibly carrying us into the playoffs. Everyone seemed to have written me off. With my two pound Lenox-Hill brace holding my knee together, and cortizone killing as much of the pain as possible, I proceeded to muster every ounce of strength I could to prove the critics wrong. I was used to playing with pain, and I thought it would take a lot more to stop me. Though the pain was horrible, I kept running with the bad knee and accepting the pain. During the warm-ups of our fiftieth game, the pain reached a point I couldn't bear. The muscles had atrophied. It was impossible to continue with torn ligaments and torn cartilage. I stopped playing that night and ended my hopes of helping the Jazz make it to the playoffs.

When the season ended, the Jazz had fallen only one game short of making it to our first post-season appearance!

22

Mentally Crippled

Fan letters had poured in to me constantly since the day I entered the professional ranks, and during my period of rehabilitation the letters of encouragement and sympathy arrived all the more. Most of them were a welcome distraction as I labored through therapy, but letters that spoke of people praying for me rubbed me the wrong way. As I read the words regarding prayer and God, I wadded the stationery and tossed it away in rejection.

I worked hard to redevelop the action I once had in my knee; but considering the extent of the damage, it wasn't easy. My struggle to regain physical dexterity was entwined with my mental condition, and it was a near impossibility for me to find things to lift my spirits. The media buried me soon after the injury, and the skeptics were ready to write me off forever when they learned I required surgery and a lengthy rehabilitation.

While their fiery darts were flung at me, I found my family a great encouragement. Dad especially understood the turmoil I was suffering. In his estimation not many players had been forced to endure more in a career than I had. Of course, his opinion was strongly biased; but he spoke from his heart and from our experiences together. The rehab time gave us time to air a lot things that had been on our minds for a long time. Dad admitted that during the years at LSU he had covered for me many times with the media, especially regarding my personal situation. When I was beaten down, taking the weight of losing upon myself, he handled the newspapers, making sure my public image was unsoiled, because he knew the importance of the proper perception of the fans. Dad also knew how insecure I had been since grade school, especially through the early days when I fumbled through conversations and avoided girls and social situations. Dad again wanted to protect me.

Seeing me disabled physically and worn mentally troubled him a great deal. It hurt him to see me without my customary dedication to the game, the dedication that had taken me so far. To Dad it was just a matter of healing the knee and getting back in action despite what critics were saying.

I wished it were that simple. My life was unstable, and the desire for stability and peace had never been greater. I hated the thought of going back to the back stabbing and hypocrisy in professional sports, but the obsession of winning the championship ring still persisted and haunted me. How could I abandon a dream that had begun even before my birth? I had to win that ring; and if I ended the pursuit prematurely, I knew I would have to live with the decision the rest of my life.

I gathered all the strength I could and overcame the odds to get my knee back into good shape. I felt ready to go as I reported to practice. The doctor fitted me with a special two pound Lenox-Hill brace to help stabilize my knee. However, though the brace protected my knee and allowed me to run down court, it virtually prohibited any lateral movement. In essence, the brace became my knee, allowing all the muscle to atrophy. Psychologically, I became addicted to wearing it and depended on its support instead of rehabilitating the muscles and tendons to their original state. Despite the physical pain and discomfort, I averaged almost twenty-three points a game for the first half of the season.

By midseason I could feel my knee weakening with every game, and the doctors and I realized that I hadn't allowed enough time for the injury to heal after the surgery. With thirty games remaining in the season and the Jazz without any hopes of going to the playoffs, all involved agreed that I should take the rest of the season off to let my knee heal properly.

During the off-season my knee finally began to come around. I look back in retrospect and think how foolish I was even to play the 1978–79 season, but hindsight is always good. By the fall of 1979 my knee had grown strong enough to take off the brace.

With my knee healing, it seemed as though nothing could stand in the way of my quest for a championship. But, one event that I didn't anticipate was the New Orleans Jazz being sold and relocated to Utah. With the change of location and ownership came change of management and the hiring of a new coach.

I remember the first game for Utah vividly. I had about four points in the first couple of minutes of the game when suddenly it hit me; I had no excitement for the game. Obviously our team would suffer through another struggling year—another rebuilding year. Mentally I didn't have the enthusiasm to survive that kind of season. Most of all, I didn't want to face another losing season with each loss being placed on my shoulders.

We played San Diego at home for the fifth game of the season and won for the first time as the Utah Jazz. I scored twenty-eight points to lead all scorers, but deep inside I felt no satisfaction with the effort because I knew another losing season was inevitable.

The seventeenth game of the year found us at home playing the Los Angeles Lakers, who boasted of their great rookie, Ervin "Magic" Johnson. Because of the obvious potential for media hype, the game was promoted as "The Magic Men" meeting head-to-head.

Despite the media build-up, complete with posters of Magic and me, the heralded match never took place. I walked into the locker room that night and watched our coach write a surprising line-up on the blackboard—with my name missing. The humiliation I felt was almost overwhelming. Thousands of my fans came to see me play, and I had to sit in disgrace on the bench. Oddly enough, I didn't ask the coach why I was omitted from the line-up; and he didn't bother to explain. Later I found out the Jazz management had basically gone along with the coach's decision to get rid of me—a very unpopular decision with me, to say the least! I made my feelings known to the owner, but it was to no avail. He told me he needed to go with his coach's judgment.

Being benched was a difficult thing to live with. My pride was shattered. I never saw myself as someone who would sit and watch. I guess other players empathized with me, knowing how hard it was. They may have even thought my coach's choices were wrong, but a player doesn't complain too much and expect to last long in professional sports.

For two months I dressed out and sat on the bench every game.

The frustration and bitterness showed up in many sleepless nights. I still had to go to practice and go through the motions of being a professional basketball player, and the humiliation I felt bore a rebellious attitude. I let it be known in no uncertain terms that I would play, or the Jazz would pay.

One night, in an emotional call to my dad, I poured out my feelings and told him I felt like I was mentally crippled. I expressed my hurt to him, telling him I could not continue as I had, and I was ready to throw what talent I had to the wind and forget basketball forever! Dad steered the conversation toward the positive and discussed my options, including landing a spot on another ball club. We agreed I would be wasting what time I had left if I landed a spot on just any team that would have me. I wanted to have one last shot at winning a championship ring!

On January 18, 1980, I was officially released by the Utah Jazz. After I worked out a settlement concerning my contract, I technically became a free agent seeking a job with another team in the league. Unfortunately, rumors had been spread that I couldn't play anymore. Those who chose to believe the story made a completely false assumption.

False or not, when rumors are spread one can do little to combat them. In my case I compared spreading the rumor to taking a feather pillow to the top of the Empire State Building and dumping out all the feathers. Of course, the down would be scattered in every direction, as far as one could see. I could walk through the streets of New York trying to retrieve every single feather and put the pillow back together, but it would be impossible to find them all and restore the pillow. Such was the nature of the rumors regarding my ability. Once they were out there, they couldn't be retrieved.

With the rumors circulating not many teams came knocking at my door. I was regarded as a hot potato and nobody really wanted to touch me no matter how well I could play. Admittedly, though, my immaturity helped me mishandle the situation completely. When I was benched I never said anything to the press, and often that's the worst thing a pro athlete can do. In my case, I wanted desperately to avoid a spitting contest; so instead of just saying what I believed and getting it over with, my pride got the best of me and I held it all inside. Ironically, the owners commended me for my attitude and praised me for not going to the papers. If only they had known how my silence was eating away at me. I look back now and realize how I let my outward circumstances tear my insides apart. From where I stood I had no foundation on which to fall back. I was miserable, and I had bitterness and hate within me. I just wanted to leave the situation and go prove myself elsewhere, as I had done all my life.

But, I wasn't exactly sought after when I was released. Finding out you're not as hot as you think you are really gives a guy a jolt. I couldn't understand the disinterest considering I was only thirty-one at the time, hardly over the hill!

I persisted in my search and narrowed my choices to Philadelphia and Boston—two teams destined for championships. Philly wanted me to have my knee examined since they too had heard the rumors of a knee problem. This request discouraged me, but after a doctor's careful examination, he announced to the Sixers that my knee was fine. Of course, it wasn't totally fine. I couldn't play forty minutes a game without it swelling since I had never really let it heal properly. But the knee was strong enough to play at least half a game on a nightly basis.

Though I passed the physical exam for Philly, I chose Boston, the highest bidder. Of course, the money was all relative considering both teams weren't offering much more than minimum league salaries. The negotiation table had changed a lot since I had first signed with the league. But the money wasn't my main concern at the time and I was quick to tell Boston's general manager, Red Auerbach, exactly that.

He wanted to give me a two-year contract and foolishly I said no, because I wanted to prove to him and everyone that I could still play. I thought if I won them over with my performance, then we would talk about the next year. I needed to prove to myself I could still play because I knew that mentally I was in no condition to do so. I had allowed all the negative aspects of my situation to totally weigh me down. To me, basketball had to be more than just a physical act. I felt mentally crippled and knew I needed some type of enthusiasm if I were going to continue playing.

I really had physically abused myself with stress over the previous two months. That, combined with all my drinking, nearly destroyed me. Though I didn't realize it fully, I had set my life's foundation on sand and was being washed away by every wave. Despite the instability of the situation, I knew if ever I could find a place to get a shot at the championship and get back the enthusiasm for the dream I had possessed as a kid, it was Boston.

23

Walking Away

The 1979–80 season was half over when I carried my duffle bag into Boston Garden, where all of a sudden, I found myself in the hallowed hall of champions. I looked up to the ceiling of Boston's arena and saw the evidence of the franchise's long tradition of winning basketball games. Banners from championships gone by filled the rafters.

The Celtics were a team that knew how to win. Though I had always been labeled a maverick and a hot dog, I had always longed to play with a group of players who worked as one cohesive unit. My critics found it hard to believe that was my desire.

When I arrived I knew I wasn't going to be a starter, and that was fine with me, because playing half of each game was all I wanted out of Boston. The Celtics were loaded with great players, including Robert Parrish, Larry Bird, Dave Cowens, and Nate Archibald. I even asked mangagement to let me prove myself on the court before making any long-term agreements. The important thing to me was the fact that I was on a good team. I wanted to be able to contribute wherever I could, and that seemed to be understood when I was told I would play at least a half. Unfortunately, that never took place.

I found out that my new teammates weren't too enthusiastic about me joining their club. Like me, they had a great deal of pride. Boston was already winning and I had a legacy of playing on losing teams. Why did they need Pete Maravich?

In the beginning I couldn't concern myself with the pride of others. I had quite a bit of physical and mental conditioning to undertake before I could resume playing. The discouraging time in Utah had left me undisciplined. But with a new contract in hand, I was ready to begin working immediately to get myself back into shape.

My rejuvenation period took on some weird characteristics of its own. After a press conference announcing my arrival to the Celtics, I was removed from sight. For the first two weeks in Boston I never saw any of the other players! I had to practice in another gym with one of the people from the front office. That was how they expected me to get in shape. I knew the only way I could get in shape for NBA competition was to play against other professional players. The team's actions didn't make any sense to me. When I pressed for an explanation I was told they needed to bring me into the system slowly. That's when I remember feeling as though I was some kind of an alien or a disease for which they needed to find a cure.

I did everything they asked me to, but the circumstances were hauntingly similar to what had happened in Atlanta when I was asked to go to New Orleans. A lot of promises were made but most never came to fruition. I did play a little with the Celtics and my time was even increased on the court here and there, but never to half the game as I had been told.

The highlight of the season came when I started two games. One of the regular starters had a death in the family, and because of his misfortune I was informed I would step in for him. I had over thirty points the first night and after the game the press surrounded me. But what should have been a triumphant moment became the worst thing that could have happened: the other players thought I was infringing upon them since they had paid their dues to make Boston a winner, and all of a sudden *I* was getting the attention. Honestly, all I ever wanted to do was play the game, avoid the attention, and go home. In fact that night I hardly mentioned to the reporters how I played, trying hard to just mention the team and the total effort. But, I could do nothing about what they reported. I knew I had dug myself into a deeper hole.

The next night we played the Detroit Pistons, and by half time I had scored twenty points and we were winning big. I wasn't doing anything special, just playing Celtic ball. I couldn't help but score with our fast-breaking ability. I started the second half but played sparingly. In my two nights as a starter I was the team's leading scorer, and we won each game. The next day, the starting player returned, and I went back to playing my ten to twenty minutes. I understand the coach was in a very delicate situation and like any team, he had to polish the egos of all the players there before me.

Despite my season's average of twelve points per game, with fewer than eighteen minutes on the court per game, I sat on the bench during the playoffs. Ironically, we met the team I turned down earlier that season, the Philadelphia Seventy-Sixers and Julius Erving. The Sixers went on to win the NBA championship. I sat on the bench with my legs crossed and watched us lose four games out of five. Again, my hopes for a championship ring slid down the drain.

The off season became a time to reflect on how close I had come to completing my dream. But, the confusion and disappointment were happily interrupted by the birth of our first baby. Jackie gave birth to a beautiful little boy. We named him Jaeson. I could hardly take my eyes off the little miracle who entered our lives. He was so innocent and wonderful.

About that time I thought of leaving the game, not because of the obvious attraction of a serene home life but rather a combination of feelings I had as I considered the championship ring.

All my life I had depended on the game of basketball and considered it the constant and ultimate supplier of all my needs. The game fed me, clothed me, brought me acceptance in society, and paid my fare to every place I wanted to go. A diamond ring and its significance would cap off years of dedication to my provider. But, I started thinking how empty I would have been if Boston had won the 1980 championship while I had been sitting on the bench. Would I have been satisfied with a ring I had not helped win?

Also, I thought about what would happen after the championship was won. What would I do? Where would I go? What if the championship ring didn't fill the vacuum I felt in my life? Would I have no goal in life? Would I even have a reason to live?

These conclusions were extreme, but at the time they were typical thoughts. My existence was based on reaching the top and being the very best. Once I reached the apex, what more could I try for? I carried these thoughts into training camp the fall of 1980.

My teammates arrived at camp full of optimism, knowing the

Celtics had the tools to turn our fortunes around and bring the championship trophy back to Boston. Nineteen-eighty was the one that had gotten away, and it would not happen again.

I should have been caught up in the optimistic fervor when I arrived, but I couldn't stop thinking about what might happen if we made it all the way to the playoffs again and I had spent the year on the bench in disgrace. There were no guarantees. Even worse was the thought of what I would do if I won the ring. I firmly believed my future would be empty after that experience.

The thoughts were disturbing to me, but I couldn't express my feelings to any of the other players. I kept my chin up and continued practicing every day as if nothing were wrong.

Pride and fear of what the future held eventually got the best of me as we neared the preseason action. I suited up as usual before scrimmage and picked up a basketball. As I dribbled onto the court with the rest of the players, the applause began. The sounds of the fans seemed eerie and did not affect me as they had for the last twenty-three years. The whistles and shouts were lost high in the rafters instead of penetrating my soul.

I was participating in Boston's traditional Green and White scrimmage, and all eyes were dissecting the quality and depth of the team favored to win the world championship. I waited for the usual feeling of adrenaline to come over me as I took the floor. Slowly it came and I started playing hard. Up and down the court I ran, looking for play making opportunities, my instincts taking over.

Final seconds ticked off the clock, and I racked up thirty-eight points for the preseason contest. The team had cause for elation when we entered the locker room. The Celtics were strong and already showing impressive signs of being the team to watch all the way to the final game, but for me personally I had my doubts.

Just like the previous season, the reporters came to me to get my reaction. I fielded all their questions as best I could, down-playing my performance, then I showered.

When things started to die down in the locker room, I was told of the remarks coming from the coaching staff regarding my thirty-eight point performance. Evidently, they thought I still had a long way to go before becoming a true Boston Celtic.

Their words had a familiar ring. I sat down near my locker. This was it; I knew the time had come to stop playing. My career was over. Dad would get no satisfaction that his son would one day be recognized as one of the world's five best. I would never play on a championship team. The third goal in the inherited dream would never become a reality.

On that cold fall night in Boston I walked away from the dream. The Celtics went on that season to win the world championship.

24

Recluse

Without a doubt, the plane ride from Boston to New Orleans was the most agonizing trip of my life. Twenty-six years of living for basketball abruptly came to an end. Suddenly, I found myself at age 33 with an abundance of time to explore other interests and get my mind off the disappointment of never reaching my ultimate goal.

One by one I packed trophies and memorabilia into boxes. Everything that reminded me of basketball was moth-balled and put out of sight in storage or simply given away.

I made a clean break from basketball, granting no television or newspaper interviews. I was resolved to the fact that life is made up of choices, and it was time to begin living with the consequences of my choice to quit.

For two years I remained in seclusion, trying to wean myself from the effects of basketball. At first quitting seemed an easy proposition, but I soon discovered that leaving basketball cold turkey was the most difficult thing I had ever done. I envisioned my retirement as lazy afernoons sipping cold drinks poolside; instead I found myself wrapped in depression and self pity, wondering what to do with all the time on my hands.

The time gave me more opportunity to ponder my existence and question the huge void left in my life since walking away from the game I worshiped. I began trying to fill the emptiness with my family, especially my two-year-old son Jaeson. I figured if I could be father of the year and husband of the year, I could find the happiness and peace of mind I longed for.

I had never applied myself to academics since I considered school merely a steppingstone to playing in the NBA, but that

187

wouldn't prohibit me from personally educating my boy. I was determined that things would be much different for Jaeson.

Unfortunately, being super father and super teacher didn't have the satisfying effect I thought it would. Though I experienced some moments of enjoyment with my son, I realized I was still leading a roller-coaster existence of being happy one moment and depressed the next. My life had no consistency or purpose.

On one hand I wanted to be the perfect role model for my child, but on the other hand I saw the hypocrisy in my home life. Dad had always made it clear to me that my role off the court was more important than on the court, and I had paid lip service to the concept, turning down beer commericals and questionable movie roles that might portray a negative image to children looking up to me; but in my personal life I continued to do as I pleased.

It wasn't until I started throwing myself into Jaeson's world that I realized how much being a role model could affect my son. I knew my drinking could be a stumbling block, and it was the first thing abolished from our home life. But it was hypocritical to clean up things inside our home, such as alcohol, when I continued drinking outside.

Jackie was extremely patient as she saw the struggle I had trying to be a good father, knowing I was attempting to overcome my past failures. She tolerated my hermit-like lifestyle for weeks at a time, hoping it would soon pass like so many of my other fads had.

Before long I began using my abundance of time to worry about business deals. I decided to take control of my investments and attempt to build upon my little empire of money. I became a student of the business section of the newspaper, keeping an eye on commodities and stocks to make sure my investments were safely sheltering me and my family. If prices improved, I became ecstatic, sharing the good news with Jackie. But if prices happened to slip, I was on edge, worried about losing what I had invested. I became obsessed with keeping what I had earned.

I felt that money and things it could buy in this world were my tickets to pleasure and happiness. But even with all the money, I was miserable. Deep down I knew life had to be more than parties, a Mercedes, and stocks and bonds.

I had the money and I had the time, but with too much of both on my hands, I drove Jackie crazy with wild ideas and strange obsessions. I was preoccupied with nutrition, ordering hundreds of dollars of vitamins and filling our refrigerator with natural foods. After reading survivalist periodicals, I had the idea of building a bomb shelter. If I was going to eat healthy foods and live to be 150 years old, I didn't want my plans ruined by a nuclear bomb.

I couldn't tell how paranoid and fatalistic about my future I was becoming, and I couldn't see the unsettled individual I had become since leaving basketball. Questions about my purpose in life bombarded me: "Why am I here? What were all the years in basketball about, especially since they turned out so empty?" My mind was full of hard questions, but with all my searching, I found no answers.

Considering all the so-called good things that had happened in my life, I realized they were almost all brief interludes of ego gratification. Nothing lasted through all the accolades and trophies. I had found nothing to hang on to that would last forever. Even my greatest records would someday be broken. The trophies were collecting dust in the attic. And one day no one would remember or even care about a floppy-socked basketball player named Pistol Pete Maravich.

The fame and fads were all temporary and fleeting! My explorations of different religions, astrology, astronomy, nutrition, UFO's, and even basketball only revealed all the more an emptiness I couldn't fill.

I became a desperate man, facing the inevitable questions each person must face: "What do I have to live for? What value do I have? What will happen to me when I die?" I hadn't found a purpose anywhere in a past filled with success, fame, and fortune. For a man that seemed to have it all, in my estimation I had no purpose . . . no reason for being.

BOOK SIX

HEIR OF SALVATION

—————— **25** ——————

Lift Thine Own Heart

On a cool November evening in 1982, a chilling wind blew across Lake Pontchartrain as I sat watching television. I stared at the television screen, but my mind wandered far from the late movie. It was a time for introspection; a time for contemplating my past. Jaeson had long since been tucked into bed, and Jackie had turned in some time later.

For the most part this night was like every other night. I was living the good life, with every material thing I wanted; and I had a family who loved me. But the loneliness and guilt I felt was devastating.

Dad and Diana had been in touch by phone, concerned about my moodiness and silence; but not even a heart-to-heart talk with Dad had calmed the inner struggle.

I quietly slipped into bed and tried to close my eyes. It was useless. The harder I tried to forget what was on my mind, the more graphic my imagination became. Dark and haunting images from the past surfaced. Try as I might, those images couldn't be dismissed.

The second hand moved slowly on the alarm clock. It was 2 a.m. My head pounded with activity, a myriad of thoughts racing through my mind. My conscience was bothering me as never before. At times I thought I might be dozing off, but a glance at the alarm clock showed that the hands had moved only a minute or two.

I recalled the night I had taken my first drink on the steps of the church, and how that first sip nearly ruined my life. I considered the effect it had on my mother and on our family in general. I remembered all the ugly things I'd done to people, and I recalled the friends and enemies I had made in college and in the pros. My thoughts wandered to all the rebellion I had toward God, my family, and others. All the horrible things I had said and the stupid things I had done seemed to be illuminated. No matter how hard I tried, I couldn't derail the thoughts.

Finally, I recognized that it was more than just thoughts running through my head. It was sin.

The night wore on, and as early morning approached, I knew I had to make things right with God. As I turned to find a comfortable position in the bed, I realized the sheet was soaked with my sweat. Again, I glanced at the clock that now read 5:40 a.m. The guilt from the past was relentless and had become too heavy to handle alone, so I broke the silence with a prayer. The course my life had taken through the years had always clashed with the way God had intended, and it was time to admit it.

I cried out to God, saying, "I've cursed you and I've spit on you. I've mocked you and used your name in vain. I've kicked, punched, and laughed at you. Oh, God can you forgive me, can you forgive me? Please, save me, please. I've had it with this life of mine. I've had it with all the world's answers for happiness. All of it, the money, fame, and things have left me so empty."

I remembered the late sixties and the day in California when I rejected the idea of a personal relationship with Jesus Christ because of what it might do to interfere with my career goals. Now, sixteen years later, I wondered if God had forsaken me because of all the things I had done or not done. A deafening silence filled the dark room, and the tears I felt flowing down my cheeks were the tears of a spiritually broken man.

Suddenly, without warning, I heard a voice say, "Be strong. Lift thine own heart." The voice seemed to reverberate throughout the room. I looked up in shock and checked to see if Jackie and I were still alone. The only sound I heard was the loud thumping of my racing heart. What I'd heard hadn't come from within me. It was an audible voice!

I immediately awoke Jackie, startling her in the process. She was afraid someone was breaking into the house. "Did you hear what God said to me? You had to hear it!" I told her. "He said 'Be strong. Lift thine own heart.' "

To my surprise, she reacted as if nothing out of the ordinary had happened. She closed her eyes and lay back on her pillow. "I didn't hear a thing, Pete," she answered in a sleepy voice muffled by the pillow.

Jackie had been through so many roller-coaster experiences with me and my searching. To her my exclamation was nothing more than another wacky result of looking for my purpose in life. She figured it too would pass. She was really more interested in catching up on the sleep she was missing.

But this experience was so different from the rest! As I sat there in my excitement, I again recalled that day in California when I had rejected Christ. I recalled how my friend had received Christ into his life.

I prayed a simple prayer as best I could. "Jesus Christ, come into my life...forgive me of my sin. I believe with all my heart that you died for me and rose from the grave so I would have eternal life. Make me the person you want me to be."

Through this simple act of surrender, the void that once loomed so large was filled. From that moment on, my life was never to be the same.

26

Building The House

The transformation in my life was astonishing. Because of my new-found faith a new Pete had miraculously emerged with joy and a purpose for meaningful existence. My family could hardly believe they were seeing the same person they had known. I finally knew there was a reason for my being alive, and the assurance translated peace into my face and my attitude.

Jackie remained skeptical of my born-again experience, simply because she had firsthand knowledge of how my behavior was affected by changes that were temporary and fleeting. Everything I had attempted to study and adopt in the past such as TM, yoga, or Eastern religions reminded her that this spiritual regeneration also would fall quickly by the wayside. Jackie doubted the durability of my latest "religion." I understood her doubting, and I knew that only time could help her and the rest of my family grasp my inner transformation. I was so happy that Jesus Christ had come home into my heart replacing my restless, self-centered nature with a peace and love beyond my finite explanation.

Before that unforgettable night, I had searched long and hard for answers to the true meaning of life. I had opened many books on religion but not the Bible—the book that had the answers to all my questions.

The Bible told me that to enter the kingdom of heaven, all I had to do was have faith in Jesus. I couldn't earn it or work my way there. I couldn't get there by being ethical or full of integrity. I couldn't even be super honest to earn my way in. I certainly couldn't buy my way in with all my money and material wealth. There was simply nothing I could do to gain entrance into heaven because it was already done for me by Jesus Christ who came and died on the cross, shedding his blood for all of us to have the opportunity to accept the free gift.

Now I know I'm not here on this earth to intellectualize what the Bible says or to defend it. I'm to just stand on every word God breathed into the Bible and let it influence me, then share with people the Bible's truth and mystery. The apostle Paul said, "Christ in you, the hope of glory." That's where the mystery lies—*Christ in me.*

After that night I wanted to please God in every way I could. I started by going to church and reading the Bible constantly. Our family continued to grow as God blessed Jackie and me with another baby boy. We named him Joshua. Bringing a new life into the world took on new meaning for me. I saw my responsibility as a Christian father to raise both my boys in a different way.

As a young Christian, I wanted to build my relationship with Jackie and the boys on the foundation of God's word. I desired to grow spiritually in order to educate and instruct my sons in the power and principles of the Word of God. I also believed God would balance me in all areas of my life as I followed him and was obedient.

The months passed and we planned a move to the north shore of Lake Ponchartrain. For several years Jackie and I had agreed that if the opportunity arose we would pull up stakes and find a country atmosphere in which to raise our family. When we purchased a rustic old home in Covington, Louisiana, our goal began to become a reality.

The house we purchased was nearly one hundred years old and in need of a great deal of work. But we knew that once it was restored, it would fit our wants ideally. The house was in walking distance of schools, churches, grocery stores, hospitals, and antique stores—the latter being Jackie's favorite. The community itself had much to offer, including fresh air and water ranked as some of the best in the world and an abundance of pine and oak trees. We felt comfortable with our decision to move, and the refurbishing began.

As construction continued, I accepted an invitation to tour the Far East with nine other ex-NBA players. The trip included visits to China, Taiwan, Hong Kong, and the Philippines. The tour consisted of six exhibition games and several clinical demonstrations. Again, basketball was the key to opening doors of friendship. Incidentally, we won all our games. With the talent of players such as Rick Barry and Earl "the Pearl" Monroe, our experience was victorious over our opponents' youthful determination.

I returned home exhausted. The twenty hours of flying did me in. But the instant I saw my family the fatigue disappeared. All I wanted to do was hug and kiss them all. After a couple of recuperation days we decided to drive to our new house to check on the progress. The morning drive was beautiful; the air was cool and the sky was bright with sunshine. We were reminded of all the trips of the past few years to the little community in the country. We often had stopped for picnics or looked at potential houses to purchase. On this day we were all excited to see the progress on our new home.

The house was in the final stages of restoration. Before allowing the boys out of the car we made it very clear that they were to stay close to us, knowing how the children's curiosity is heightened in places such as construction sites. I led the tour around the outside of the house, then I took them inside and through the rooms, describing how each one would look when we moved in the furniture and called the place home. As expected tools, scrap boards, and debris were scattered everywhere; a perfect lure for a four-year-old and a two-year-old. The large front porch and the enlarged rooms captured the boys' attention and they quickly discovered fun places to play.

While exploring the downstairs, our new neighbors came over and joined us as we reviewed the progress.

As we reached the stairway, we noticed the banisters hadn't been attached. Jackie and I gripped the boys' hands tightly, and everyone climbed the stairs to the second floor. When we reached the top, I kept Joshua and Jaeson a few feet away from the unprotected stairway. We continued describing to our neighbors-to-be the plans we had for decorating the rooms, when unknown to us, the boys wandered a few feet away to do some exploring of their own. Both boys walked innocently into a tiny closet. What none of us saw was the open air duct from the old air conditioning vent, positioned like an animal trap to snare any unsuspecting person who might step onto the section of pink insulation covering its gaping hole. As I continued describing our plans for the unfinished rooms, Joshua moved closer to the opening. We were unaware of his movements and oblivious to the impending danger innocently disguised as a section of insulation.

In an instant Joshua stepped onto the insulation, which gave way, opening a hole that swallowed his tiny body and sent him plummeting one and a half floors down to the hardwood floor of the master bedroom. Jackie and I heard the thump of Josh's little head. In a flash I ran down the stairs and found Josh quiet, his head resting in a puddle of blood. My eyes focused on the amount of visual damage he had sustained. The upper side of his right cheek, eye, and forehead were all grossly misshapen, and the tremendous impact had caused his right eye to swell shut. He was barely recognizable. I heard Jackie screaming upstairs as I knelt to check his vital signs. I could barely feel his pulse, and he did not move. My only thought was that I was in the midst of a life-and-death situation and the outcome was in the hands of God.

Instincts took over as I picked up Joshua's limp body and headed out the door to the car. I didn't want Jackie and Jaeson to see how Josh looked, just in case he was dying or if he were already gone. That horrible sight could linger in their minds for the rest of their lives. I didn't want that to happen.

A neighbor saw me running to the car and offered to hold Josh as I drove to the hospital. As we left for the emergency room, Jackie ran into the front yard and watched us speed away.

The hospital was only minutes away, but the drive seemed endless, each second an eternity. When we reached the hospital I ran with Joshua into the emergency room where a doctor and a nurse immediately analyzed his condition. The blow to the head was severe, and the doctor quickly summoned an eye specialist to examine the damage to Josh's eye. Within a few minutes an eye surgeon was at Josh's side assessing the injury. The initial reaction was negative as the expert gazed into Josh's glassy eyeballs. He believed muscles had been torn away, and extensive surgery would be required to repair the right eye. At the very least Josh probably would lose his sight in one eye, and only time would tell about any brain damage.

As the doctors assessed the damage, I could only stand by and wait. I chose to believe with all my heart that the will of God would be done, and regardless of the outcome, I courageously would accept whatever the doctors told me. My faith was being tested. I realized quickly I could do very little to control every circumstance in my life; I had to believe God was in total control.

Joshua looked so pitiful lying on the hospital bed oblivious to what had occurred and to what was happening. After several more minutes of close examination the doctor told me that Joshua would live. When I heard the doctor's words I had no doubt that a miracle was taking place. He went on to explain the seriousness of the eye injury. It looked as though some muscles had been torn away, and extensive surgery would be required to save Josh's vision. Despite the grim prognosis, I felt relieved knowing Josh was going to survive the ordeal and would soon be out of danger. Then, to everyone's relief, Joshua regained consciousness and tried to focus his eyes. His head was terribly swollen, giving him a peculiar appearance, but at that moment I couldn't care less about appearance; my child was alive! The fall had nearly killed Josh, but God's mercy was on us, and he was giving us back our son!

A few more minutes passed and the doctors gave me even greater and miraculous news. On second inspection of Joshua's eye, the specialist said it was as clear as a bell and totally unaffected by the fall. For some reason the damage they had detected in the first observation no longer existed.

I was immediately humbled. Joshua could have been killed, or at least paralyzed, but according to the doctors he should walk away from it all completely normal. I was touched beyond comprehension, and so thankful that God had spared our son. A man who fears the Lord is blessed. That doesn't mean I'm scared; it means I am in awe of Him, and believe me I was when He saved my boy.

Scientists say there must be over one hundred billion stars in our galaxy, and we know the Creator has a name for every one of them. They guess that the universe has eight to ten billion more galaxies like ours with billions more stars. I cannot possibly comprehend God with my little finite brain. I can only trust and depend on my great Creator, as I did through Joshua's accident.

This was the first real test of my faith since turning my life over to

Jesus Christ. The old Pete would have wallowed in self-pity, then headed to the nearest bar to try and drown the sorrow. But, the transformed Pete Maravich lay calmly on a hospital bed near his son remembering the words in the Bible; "We know that all things work together for good to those who love God, to those who are called according to His purpose."

Jackie reached the emergency room minutes after I did. At first we didn't see each other. Jackie merely saw doctors and nurses standing quietly around the bed. The silence seemed to confirm her fear that Joshua was dead. Then Josh cried out, and I looked and saw Jackie. I shared the incredible news, and we embraced and celebrated together. I will never forget that wonderful moment.

I spent the day next to Joshua, praying and thanking God for saving our son! Josh whimpered over and over, "Dada, hurt . . . Dada, hurt." I fought back the tears as he writhed in pain. The vision of the accident and the sound of his tiny cry will never leave me. They serve as a reminder that my life is nothing without God. We are powerless and helpless without him.

There were no lasting side effects from the fall that should have claimed Joshua's life.

27

Growing Closer

One of the first things I realized after I had settled
things with God was the difference it made to be dedicated to
something other than myself. Everything I had done since childhood was for selfish reasons, such as bringing adoration to myself,
finding acceptance among my peers, and gratifying my ego. This
selfishness had led to emptiness and no conventional way out of
my self-centered way of life. Trying to please others had brought
me frustration, a drinking habit, and a love of material possessions.
I had gone to the brink of self-destruction.

After my conversion that special night in Metairie, Louisiana, I
turned full circle. All the fame and fortune I had accumulated
looked extremely pale when compared to the abundance of Christ
in me. I was driven by a desire to please God because of the
newness of life I had received from him. The fears I had once
possessed were wiped away; I became much more open to people.
The solemn moods that had plagued me began to disappear. Instead my life was now filled with the light and love of Christ.

Never was my new attitude more apparent than in May of 1985
when Dad and I were invited to Israel to do a clinic for the federa-
tion of basketball coaches. Eleven years had gone by since our last
overseas trip.

The trip was set up by an old friend, Haskell Cohen, the former
publicity director of the NBA. We were to instruct the Israeli
coaches in offensive and defensive strategies to help them get their
teams on an international level of play. We were given five days to
work the miracle.

Dad saw the trip as an opportunity to get me back into basketball, despite the fact that I had done some teaching at a clinic the

summer before and had made the trip to the Far East with the ex-NBA stars. I decided to go partly because of Dad's urging, but mostly because I wanted to visit the Holy Land. With my new-found knowledge of Jesus Christ, I considered the trip a pilgrimage.

All the arrangements were in order, and the welcoming party in Israel was prepared for the arrival of the father and son team plus our traveling companion, Notch Petrovich, Dad's old friend from Logstown. But, when we reached Kennedy Airport in New York, my passport was missing. I could picture it lying on my desk back in Louisiana. I felt really stupid. At first Dad thought I was playing a practical joke, but his face turned from a smile to a frown as Notch told him I was dead serious.

Leaving my passport at home prompted one of our verbal battles, as Dad and I bantered for a moment about my forgetfulness. But all-in-all, the incident was handled in a more genteel manner than would have been done four years earlier. Our public arguments on and off the court had become legendary at LSU. What people saw back then, though, was really two Serbs expressing their feelings in a colorful manner! The disagreements had never been because of a lack of love between us.

A few minutes after our discussion I came up with a solution. I would catch a later flight once Jackie express mailed my passport to me. Meanwhile, Dad and Notch would take the original flight and wait for me in Israel. We were all frustrated we wouldn't make the flight together; but Dad agreed to the resolution, not wanting to upset things in Israel because of a late arrival.

The passport arrived from Louisiana the next day, and I hopped a plane to the Middle East. Because of delayed or canceled flights, my connecting flight included a twenty-four-hour layover in Greece, so I planned to make the best of my blunder and enjoy my visit there as well. Though I would miss the official greeting party at the Tel Aviv airport, I considered the stopover a blessing since I would get the opportunity to tour a part of the world I'd never seen.

I got off the plane in Athens, rented a hotel room, and began exploring the ancient city by taxi. The Parthenon and Acropolis were on my sightseeing list, as well as most of the other tourist attractions. With plenty of time on my hands I went back to the hotel and asked the clerk where I should eat. He directed me to some restaurants off the beaten tourist path. I wandered through the streets of the seaport, where I encountered some young children playing basketball on a playground.

As I watched the youngsters play, the temptation was too great for me to ignore. I decided to have some fun, so I walked onto the school grounds, stood under the basket and captured the attention of the kids. My 6'5" frame was a little hard to miss in a crowd of young Greek children. Even though I didn't speak a word of their language, I began communicating in a universal language—basketball.

They threw me the ball, and I began spinning it on my finger. I'll never forget the looks of the wide-eyed children. They couldn't believe what they were seeing.

I didn't have to understand their language to fully comprehend the exclamations and gasps from my young audience. I noticed a few kids running away as the others stayed to watch, wondering what was next. I continued my mini-Showtime and began dribbling. They loved one drill called punching the bag. That's where I start dribbling the ball a few inches off the ground and continue until my hands are a blurr. After the dribbling exhibition I began shooting the ball from all areas of the court.

The children who had run off returned stringing their friends and neighbors behind them. After a few minutes of interacting with the kids, I excused myself from the playground and headed back to the hotel. I left wondering if the kids and other spectators would tell their local coaches of the new basketball player in town.

If there was a lesson to learn from this encounter, it was how basketball could be used as a tool to break down communication barriers. My political or philosophical background didn't matter; people appreciated someone who had mastered a skill and entertained them.

I made my connecting flight and arrived in Tel Aviv in time for the press conference. Dad and I sat in a room as newspaper people filled the place to document the arrival of the American basketball personalities.

As always Dad took his duty to teach basketball very seriously.

During the press conference he pointed out the reasons for the clinic and what we intended to accomplish in just one week. Skepticism was evident, but it made Dad all the more determined. He continued the interview and stepped on the toes of just about everyone as he condemned the treatment of coaches in Israel and criticized the state of Israeli basketball in general.

His criticism was well-founded. Coaches in Israel had no job security, low pay, and the ever-present demand for them to win it all or be fired. They weren't given time to work on basics and build a team over a period of time; they had to start winning immediately and keep winning or they were out looking for work. Basically, the players didn't have the skills to become winners. As a result, basketball in Israel had suffered and stayed on an inferior level internationally.

We also faced some disagreement as to the content of the week-long clinic. Dad learned that the coaches attending would expect to hear only strategies concerning offense and defense, and if he wandered off into teaching fundamentals he would probably lose nearly every coach there.

That kind of attitude toward basketball made his blood boil. When he was informed of the possible response to teaching fundamentals, he said he didn't care. He knew basketball would never be great in Israel without attention to basics, and he wasn't about to leave the country without stressing them.

After the formalities and introductions, we were given one week to tour the country for sightseeing. Without a doubt this tour of the Holy Land was the highlight of my time there. As a Christian, I was humbled as I visited the places where Jesus walked; and nothing moved me more than walking into the Jordan River and trying to grasp the significance of it. As I walked out of the water, tears ran down my face, I was so overwhelmed.

After that preliminary week Dad was refreshed and primed to get started. Just as the local officials had warned, the coaches were cool to the idea of learning fundamentals. The Israeli coaches sat quietly with skeptical looks on their faces. They even huffed with impatience when Dad didn't delve immediately into game-winning strategy. Eventually, they began firing questions at Dad regarding offensive and defensive strategy. He quickly answered them all, diagramming his replies on a chalkboard. Observing from a distance, I noticed the familiar angry glare forming in Dad's eyes as he zipped through his answers. He was reading their attitudes loud and clear, so he finally stopped his instruction to shout at them.

"Listen to me!" he barked, as he grabbed a basketball. His forceful voice captured their attention. "See this basketball?" he asked. As the coaches watched skeptically, he took his chalk and angrily drew a circle the size of a dime on the surface of the ball. "Can you see that little white circle?" he shouted. "Look real close! That circle represents every ounce of knowledge I have about the game of basketball. This basketball represents all the unexplored areas of the game that I don't know!" Dad continued as he ran his hand over the sphere. Then he poked the surface of the ball with the chalk, leaving a tiny dot that no one in the audience could detect. "That dot, gentlemen, is what every one of you coaches put together know about basketball!" Dad's voice rang through the room, and judging the silence that followed, his point was driven home.

From that moment on Dad had their undivided attention. The coaches stayed to learn basic fundamentals and creative ways of learning the fundamentals, as well as all the strategies Dad had to teach them. Each day Dad started with the fundamentals, and I talked of my career and demonstrated drills to perfect fundamentals and build confidence. Then Dad answered any questions regarding strategies. He shared his knowledge regarding offenses and defenses; setting up plays; throwing the ball in bounds from different areas of the court; breaking a 1-3-1 zone, or a 2-3 zone; breaking a "box-and-one" or a "triangle and two." Whatever questions they had, Dad explained it on a chalkboard, then set up the situation on the court using players.

The week was a great success for the clinic organizers. The first day thirty to forty coaches attended. As word spread, however, we ended up teaching nearly two hundred coaches and assistants. Israeli television and radio covered the last day of the event. The clinic would have been an overall triumph for us if Dad hadn't developed an ailment during the week. A problem developed with his prostate gland. Being the trooper he was, he didn't want to bother anyone with his inconvenience or jeopardize the clinic. He kept the pain to himself while he continued on his feet every day for hours at a time. As the week wore on, his condition grew more serious, and finally he confided in me. He was passing only blood, so he finally agreed to let me call a doctor to his hotel room to examine him. The doctor gave him some pills, but the pain was unbearable. Just before a dinner honoring us, Dad found himself in a hospital emergency room.

For the first time in over thirty years, I saw my father for the mortal human being he was. As he lay on the hospital bed, in excruciating pain, I was helpless.

"There's no way he should be alive," the doctor said as I stood near the bed. The words hit me like a brick. This man had shown me everything, and to suddenly realize Dad wouldn't always be around came as a sobering blow. I contemplated the future without him, and didn't like what I saw. I thought of a number of things I still wanted to do for him and with him. Thankfully, his condition eventually stabilized enough to get him back to the States where he received care and attention from his personal physician.

Dad and I had traveled a long road together through the ups and downs of basketball and a stormy home life. Even after the arguments that had us ready to strangle each other, we emerged with total love and respect for one another. His illness made me see how much I truly loved him.

As we continued to open up to one another, our relationship grew stronger and drew us closer together. We gradually found it easier to talk about the most personal things in our lives including the disappointments, such as the toll alcohol had taken on our entire family and the disappointment of missing basketball championships.

I finally faced facts and admitted it was simply my pride and immaturity that had made me walk away from Boston's championship season. I wished I had some way to satisfy the dream Dad had for me.

Dad understood the dilemma I faced, knowing that I didn't have the desire any longer to commit myself to such a goal. But, what I never had known was the fact that I had fulfilled his dreams without ever wearing a championship ring.

Back in the late 1920s when Dad had started with a peach basket, a homemade basketball, and a vision for what the simple game could mean in the life of an individual, he had realized what effects great players could have on the sport—stars like Joe Lapchick and Dutch Denhert. And basketball was a two-way street; the more a man gave to the game, the more it seemed to give back if he tried hard enough.

The real dream Dad had from the beginning for me wasn't a piece of jewelry for my finger or the recognition that I was on the best team in the world. The dream was for us to try to push basketball to the furthest limits possible. His vision saw the basketball court as a spawning ground for physical excitement and originality. The arena was fertile ground for pitting great minds and bodies together for competition.

So, I had no reason to apologize for falling short of the diamond ring. As far as my Dad was concerned, his vision had been realized and I need not concern myself with his disappointments.

Because of the change in my life, I had been reflecting on our relationship as never before. My respect for what Dad had done for me caused me to be very open and honest with him. A year earlier I found myself recollecting the tumultuous days gone by, and the haunting memory of the NIT entered my mind. I still felt guilty over a dozen years later for my dreadful performance and foolishness. I had blown my father's chance for a shot at a national title, not to mention my own, and to make matters worse I had never told him it was my fault. I had to make things right with Dad.

With my heart on my sleeve, I approached him and revealed the shame of my behavior the night before the semi-final game in New York City. I told him how I had stayed up all night drinking and that's why my performance was so poor that night. I told him how in my foolishness I had thought I could go out and party all night and still perform on the court. Choking back the tears, I apologized for the poor judgment that had cost LSU a shot at the National Invitational Tournament title and changed my dad's life forever.

I asked him to forgive me, and as usual he tried to brush it off as no big deal. As he laughed and told me to forget it, I said, "No, Dad. I'm serious. I will not leave this room until this is right between us."

After a pause, he replied, "Okay, Son, I forgive you." At that moment an enormous burden lifted from me, and it helped our relationship.

The confession resolved a lot of the mystery in Dad's mind regarding the tournament and laid to rest the alibis he had fabricated for his own peace of mind. He had blamed it on himself for so long.

Being a Christian, I had to concern myself with disappointments in his life that had nothing to do with me. I loved my dad and I wanted him to have the same peace Jesus Christ had given me. For years Dad had kept a great deal of bitterness in his heart regarding my mother's debilitating alcoholism, raising my little sister alone, being fired at LSU, taking the first job he could find and having it not work out. His bitterness had taken a great toll on his attitude, and I couldn't stand by and watch it continue eating away at him. I began telling him he just couldn't harbor such bitterness anymore, all the stuff he had suffered through was done.

Because of the change that had happened in my life, Dad began to see that Christianity was something lasting and real.

I don't believe anyone will go to hell because of sin. Sin was paid for in full by Jesus Christ on the cross. If someone goes to hell it's because of unbelief. I wanted Dad to believe. At the time, Dad couldn't comprehend a God so full of love that he could be forgiven for all the bitterness he had toward others. He didn't believe God would accept someone like him. I simply told him that's where I was for so long. I was in the same state of rebellion, rejection, and unbelief toward God. Frankly, for a long time I never felt a need for Jesus Christ because I had everything the world had to offer: money, material things, power, pleasure, I had it all! I lived in expensive houses and drove expensive cars—they all were priorities in my life. That is where my security lay.

Consequently, I never felt I had a need for Christ until my heart was opened up and I was spiritually broken. I found myself at the end of my rope and realized nothing out there would satisfy me and fill the void—the gaping hole, the bottomless pit in my life. Only Jesus could fill all the empty spaces. As the Bible puts it, "what will it profit a man if he gains the whole world, and loses his own soul? . . . What will a man give in exchange for his soul?"

A few years later Dad finally realized his need for God's love and forgiveness. He went to a church, and at the end of the service the pastor invited people to come down to the front of the auditorium and make known publicly that they wanted to turn their lives over to Jesus Christ. At first, no one came. After a second invitation, no one came. Finally, the pastor said he felt that someone in the church needed to come to Christ because it could possibly be that person's last chance. Dad felt a tugging at his heart to make the biggest decision of his life; he walked to the front of the church to give his life to Christ.

From that night on, Dad began to experience a healing of wounds that brought forth a peace that surpassed all his understanding. The mere mention of Jesus' name brought tears of joy to his eyes.

For over thirty years our main topic of discussion had been basketball strategy and fundamentals, but after Dad's conversion, we discussed reaching the highest goal of all—an eternal existence together with our Creator! As Paul the apostle said, we both would be pressing on "toward the goal for the prize of the upward call of God in Christ Jesus." We became "joint heirs with Christ."

28

Anxious For Nothing

Once I re-emerged into the public eye, many of my followers and fans from all the years of basketball demanded some explanation of what had happened to me. When I walked away from the game, I left as an athlete in the spotlight. Returning four years later, I was a man avoiding the center of attention but willing to tell what had happened.

A couple of years after I became a Christian, I received a phone call from a man I didn't really know. He had a message for me like none I had ever received. As I listened to him, he told me of a dream he had had two nights in a row. In his dream he saw me standing in front of thousands of young people, telling them my story. He wasn't sure what the dream meant, but he did feel compelled to contact me and tell me what he had experienced. Immediately, he tried to rationalize his call, telling me he wasn't crazy, but just feeling he was obeying the Lord.

I reassured him that I didn't question his sincerity or his sanity. After thanking him for the call, I prayed that if there was something to it I would receive some sort of confirmation. It occurred to me that I had never talked to anyone without a basketball in my hands, and doing banquets and the lecture circuit was the farthest thing from my mind.

A couple of weeks passed and I continued my usual routine until the phone began to ring and letters began to arrive asking me to speak to people about my story of how Christ changed my life. Without a doubt I was being shown how God wanted to use me.

As soon as it became known I had forsaken my reclusiveness, invitations came in from all over the country. Speaking on high school and college campuses gave me the platform I needed to give people the answer to the question, "Whatever happened to Pistol Pete Maravich?"

Recently, I told a gathering of seventeen thousand young people in North Carolina, "The feeling of total emptiness is no longer there. Money can buy you everything but happiness. It can pay your fare to everywhere but heaven. That's what I found out."

I paused and scanned the stadium full of young faces poised and ready to confront in their lives the same challenges I had faced. I knew the words I had for them might be the last time they heard a message of hope before experimenting with some of the avenues I had traveled.

I continued, "I also found out if you seek pleasure and happiness you'll never find it. But if you have the wisdom and obedience to seek Jesus Christ, happiness will find you."

This same message I took into prisons and reformatories around the country. One of the prison ministries invited me to speak to a particular prison, but they were quick to remind me that hardened criminals rarely react favorably to anyone who comes to give them a message of hope through Jesus Christ. Again, I found common ground through the inmates' interests and talents in basketball. Once I had their attention using my basketball drills, I could tell murderers and thieves that I too had been a type of prisoner all my life.

I reminded them that there are no scoreboards in heaven that keep tabs of the good and the bad we do. Having enough *goods* to outweight the *bads* has nothing to do with entering the kingdom of God.

Entering God's kingdom is a matter of choice. We all have a choice—the alcoholic, the drug addict, the depressed, the rich and the poor—everyone!

In the past if someone had offered me a million dollars, I would've chosen it and celebrated because of all the things I could do and all the things I could have. I've never known anyone who would turn down a million bucks. But, on the other hand, God has been trying to give eternal life, totally free, and most people have rejected the offer, saying, "I'll take the million. You can keep eternal life."

In high schools I challenged kids to dedicate themselves to their

God-given talents, urging them to unglue themselves from the television and discover areas of life in which they excel.

As the word spread that I was back in public, opportunities continued to present themselves. One of the most appealing to me was creating a unique summer basketball camp, touching not only the physical part of a player but also the mental, emotional, and spiritual parts.

I had done camps in the early seventies in New York and Pennsylvania and really enjoyed the instruction, but I wanted a camp unlike any other in the past. I asked my dad to help me design a program that would truly affect the students who devoted a week of their summer to learn the game Dad and I loved. What resulted was an intense program that dealt with the entire individual.

The originality of the camp revealed itself in many areas. The first objective would be to really teach students and have a serious impact on the level of their basketball abilities. Second, I would impress upon the campers a better way of eating. Finally, they would meet men and women whose lives were committed to Jesus Christ.

The basketball instruction is Homework Basketball, the same teaching Dad gave me as a child. We use all the drills and ball handling techniques he invented in the 1950s that helped me earn a place in the professional ranks and excel in my game.

A wealth of information is given the kids to inspire them to achieve their full potential during an actual game.

It's a thinking man's camp, orchestrated to push a player to his fullest. If a student leaves without vastly improving his ball handling, dribbling, passing, or shooting, as well as his ability to understand what's happening and how to react in a game situation, he wasn't fully conscious throughout the week!

Kids come to a basketball camp to learn to play basketball, but off the court the campers are introduced to the benefits of eating properly and taking care of the inside of their body. I want young players to know they can maximize their athletic ability and performance by maximizing what they eat.

"If you can't last four days without a soft drink or candy, you have a discipline problem," I tell my campers. "If you can't say no for four days, you may not be able to say no to more harmful things

211

in your life down the road. That kind of discipline problem will translate into your game."

My main concern is to let young people know that I am interested in them and their problems, not merely their abilities on the basketball court. Basketball has changed so much in the thirty plus years I've been involved in it. Today, more than ever, the television commercialization and media marketing of college and professional athletics has had incredible impact on kids and their families. Children's problems seemed to get lost in all the hoopla.

Because of the pursuit of entertainment dollars, the greatest impact I've seen in basketball is the phenomenal growth of technology—from instant replays to instructional videos. More camera angles and the injection of sophisticated Barnum and Bailey environments have pushed the game even further into the realm of the spectacular.

The game itself has increased in popularity because the product has been presented and promoted in a fascinating way. Athletes have used small changes, such as the encouragment to dunk and the three point play, to create for themselves a new subculture I refer to as "spectafanatics." These are the parents, ticket buyers, and sports junkies who gyrate, groan, scream, dance, shake, rattle, and roll with every new charismatic hang-in-the-air, in your face slam dunk or "slunkers," as they're known on the inner-city school grounds. The spectafanatic also encourages schools to offer scholarships to players who possess great outside shooting ability. This new breed's assignment is to enter the game and fire a rainbow missile from behind the three-point line to devastate the opposition's defense.

For whatever motive, many parents today put undue pressure on their young sons and daughters, urging them to compete and commit their lives to an unrealistic goal. Approximately one in a million children will make it to the pro basketball level, and when they get there the average stay is less than four years. That's more like a visit than a career.

Kids are unique. Some are very sensitive; others can be very aloof at times. When parents and leaders use patient instruction to encourage children's participation in a sport, the child will be more likely to respect and respond to that instruction. Screaming at a

212

seven-year-old for making a genuine mistake can lead to a future mental disaster.

I have seen the need for positive encouragement much more than the need for negative reprimand, mainly because of something I call negative absorption. I remember a particular day at one of my camps when one of my coaches informed me that a camper was hysterical and wanted to go home. He was so upset and frantic that he was having dry heaves and crying uncontrollably.

I found the boy in the cafeteria with his head in his hands and tears running down his face. I sat next to him, and after a moment I asked if anything was physically wrong. He assured me he wasn't in pain, then began sobbing through his complaints.

"I want to go home," he started. "I hate the camp, I hate the food, I hate the coaches. . . ." He went on to list almost everything but the weather. His complaints weren't new to me, and it was obvious the real problems weren't the superficial complaints he listed. After some questioning he admitted that nobody liked him. Some of the kids called him names like fatso, tubbo, and blimp. To top it off, he admitted the fact that his parents had forced him to attend the camp, and he didn't even like basketball.

The young man was a victim of negative absorption. "Let me show you something," I began. I got a glass of water and poured a little puddle on the table in front of him. Then I got two napkins and dropped one onto the puddle. "What's happening?" I asked him.

"The napkin's soaking it up," he answered as he wondered what I was up to.

"The absorption factor," I replied. I dropped the other napkin in a dry spot next to the puddle. "What happened?"

"Nothin' " he responded.

"That's right. You see, you're just like that wet napkin. All your life you've absorbed the negative, nasty, critical remarks of others. That was your choice," I said. "I'm telling you that you don't have to absorb any negative pressure. None. God doesn't make mistakes. He created you just like you are—unique." The boy's eyes widened. "There is only one of you in the entire cosmos. Don't let other kids who possess greater insecurities and ignorance drive you to buckle under negative pressure. You can be like the dry napkin—full of confidence and a desire to please God. He'll be your shield to deflect all those poison darts coming at your mind."

We had a long talk, and the change in his face told the whole story. He realized he had chosen to take the path of insecurity and vowed to stop. When he smiled, I grabbed him and hugged him. When I said, "I love you," he squeezed me tighter.

Not only did he finish the week with us, he called his family and begged to stay another. His whole attitude changed because someone reached out and shared the truth about God's love and the fact that Jesus Christ can give a person hope and new desires.

With patience and understanding, kids can endure the harsh realities of sports and life, using the former as a processing ground to combat life's constant frustrations.

No one can have complete control over all the circumstancs in his or her life, but the one aspect we can control is how we stand up and face whatever adverse circumstances come our way. Our attitude and response will declare our degree of maturity. That's one principle I want my campers to understand. The honors, fun, and all that basketball has to give will be in perspective if they understand that fact.

Not long ago, I was honored in a fashion in which I wish all my campers could be. For about three years I received requests from Sam Battisone, the owner of the Utah Jazz, to come to Salt Lake City and attend a half-time ceremony to be given in my honor for the retirement of my jersey. The organization wanted to retire my number 7 and knew it was only appropriate that I should be there when it happened. Oddly enough, the last time I had sat in the arena, my mind was on getting out of the jersey as quickly as possible. But, on December 14, 1985, I returned with my head up to receive the applause of those who knew my history and the good times we had enjoyed together on the court. The standing ovation was humbling as I accepted the framed jersey. At that moment I realized I had spent my whole career trying desperately to play on a championship team. But on this night I was being recognized as the player who helped start the franchise and helped plant the seeds that made it what it is. It was a moment of genuine appreciation, and I was deeply moved. I consider the entire event a testimony to how one can overcome negative absorption and also how Christ can help anyone overcome bitterness.

As I slowly moved back into the public realm of basketball, my son Jaeson began feeling the reverberations in the classroom. One day he came home from school and sat next to me for a heart-to-heart talk. I had been on the road speaking and doing color commentary for one of the networks, so I was good and ready to assume my fatherly duties and spend some quality time with my boys. I asked him how things were in first grade and what was on his mind. Jaeson told me of the trials and tribulations of math, then gave me a curious look.

"Daddy, did you used to be Pistol Pete?" he asked innocently.

I smiled and caressed Jaeson's straight hair. "Yes," I answered. "I guess I was. Why?"

"That's what they say at school. I just wondered," Jaeson replied, then ran off to play with Josh.

I couldn't help but think of the difference between the way Jaeson was growing up and the way Dad and Mom had raised me. By age seven I knew all about my dad's career in professional basketball.

Never was that fact more evident than the first time Jackie and I went to see Jaeson play with his school team. All the parents were there to see their offspring please them with basketball skills, and of course, a lot of eyes were on the young Maravich boy. Considering the identity of his father and grandfather, they figured Jaeson would be a ringer for sure.

Unfortunately, the opposite was true. I had not instructed Jaeson in basketball, and it was quite obvious when it came time for him to throw an inbounds pass. He stood on the court oblivious as to what he was to do. I had left my six-year-old totally unarmed and unprepared for battle.

I've never felt that Dad forced me into basketball. He planted the seeds, and I made the dream grow. I didn't want to create another basketball robot as I had been, but I did want to instill in my son some fundamentals and a competitive spirit and plant the seeds. I did so by giving my friends at the NBA a call, asking them to send me an all-star highlight film. Leah Wilcox, a friend of mine in the

NBA film department, was kind enough to send us a video.

I put the tape in my video tape machine and asked Jaeson to take a look at it. He couldn't have been more uninterested. Sensing his attitude, I told him it was all right, he didn't have to watch. I left the room and worked in my study for a couple of hours. When I returned, he was glued to the television watching the NBA video. The next few days he memorized every shot, every move, and every player's name.

I had put up two basketball goals, one for Jaeson and a shorter one for Joshua. Once the NBA tape became a part of their lives, the baskets started getting plenty of use. I instructed Jaeson in the basics of basketball, and like a duck taking to water, he began dribbling and shooting the ball naturally. Before long, he started dribbling up and down the court; down with his right hand and back up the court with his left.

Maybe he will become a fine basketball player, and maybe he won't. I only know I have learned to be "anxious for nothing," because our lives are in God's hands. When I grew up, my foundation was built on sand, and when I went the wrong way, I had nothing to come back to. No matter how interested my sons become in basketball, I know the most important foundation in their lives is the foundation of Jesus Christ. Of course, the ultimate choice is theirs to make, but I will bring them up in the way they should go and trust they won't depart from it.

29

Peace

Since I began this book, so much has transpired in my relationship with my father. I mentioned in the beginning that to tell my story would be to tell my father's story because both are so entwined. I'm not so sure I realized the importance of those words until now.

In the fall of 1986, Dad complained to his physicians about discomfort in his shoulders. After a battery of tests, he was told his body was battling bone cancer. He began undergoing radiation treatments right away. I was in touch by telephone as usual to check on him, and of course, he was still the courageous fighter he had been all his life. The end of November and the first of December tested that courage and strength, but he persevered. We both continued to pray believing God had everything in control.

December 18, I had a speaking engagement in Orlando, Florida; so I flew to Clearwater, Dad's home, and picked him up. We drove to the engagement, and even managed to attend a Christmas basketball tournament while we were there. As we drove back to Clearwater, the trip wasn't quite so pleasant. Dad had a horrible cough he had been living with for over a month. The cough, combined with the radiation therapy, had drained a good deal of his energy. I knew he was feeling terrible when he got in the back seat of the car and lay down for the remainder of the drive. That drive marked the beginning of the most difficult journey of my life.

At Christmas 1986 the entire Maravich family was planning to gather at our home for a traditional holiday. For the first time in a long while the family would be in one place at one time. Jackie's family was coming, Diana would be home from school, Ronnie was coming from New Orleans, and Dad planned to travel from Florida with me to be with the people he loved.

We were all looking forward to the time together, especially since we now truly understood the meaning of the Christmas season. Unfortunately, a shadow was silently cast upon the celebration as the seriousness of Dad's illness became know to the members of the family.

Dad's cough was worse than ever, and it was obvious to all of us that something had to be done. We called off the Christmas gathering and took him to the hospital where he was immediately diagnosed as having walking pneumonia.

The Christmas reunion was canceled, and we began caring for Dad at our house. The deterioration of his health was so quick, it seemed to be happening right before my eyes. He was prescribed ten different drugs, including medication for his cough, for the pain, to help him breathe, and for phlebitis. The doctors were doing everything they knew to help his condition, and considering the excruciating pain that the bone cancer was inflicting on him, I was deeply grateful. Unfortunately, I could see the negative effects still manifesting themselves in Dad. As I heard him cough and fight for air, the thoughts of lung cancer entered my mind. I fought those thoughts with prayers asking my heavenly Father to help us.

I'm sure Dad was a rush of emotions as he stared the gloomy forecasts in the face. In a quiet moment, he told me through tears that he regretted that his life hadn't been lived with a greater purpose. "I wish I'd been a doctor, or something like that . . . something that would've helped people," he said quietly.

I answered quickly, reprimanding him for such a ridiculous statement. I reminded him of the lives he had influenced for good all over the world and recalled the joy he brought to people's lives through his contributions to basketball. The camps, the clinics, the thousands of games in people's memories—all chapters written in thousands of lives. He will never know how many people he encouraged and helped in his lifetime. I tried to drive home to him how much he was loved and respected because of who he is.

The cancer and the rigors of therapy continued to drain Dad's trademark vitality, and all the drugs depressed his embattled immune system. Joy was hard to find. Eventually, he nearly quit eating and drinking altogether.

I began praying intensely, looking to God for some direction. In December, I had heard of a noted German doctor who was a pioneer in cancer surgery and research. After a week on my knees, I felt we had to try to get Dad to the renowned specialist, even if most people here in the States seemed to be giving up all hope. I had to remain faithful and believe in his healing.

On February 11, we headed for Hanover, Germany, though we were aware the trip itself could kill Dad. The trip was long and hard, but we made it safely to Europe. The two weeks that followed were the toughest I have ever spent. Dad was put through painful injections and treatments, but the doctor reminded us he was no miracle worker. He didn't want us getting our hopes too high. Within two days, the cough that had plagued Dad for five months disappeared. It was remarkable! Once the cough was gone and he received treatment to relieve some of the pain, Dad improved enough to manage a smile.

With rays of hope shining in his eyes, I felt it was time to talk seriously to Dad regarding the truths I had discovered in the Bible. I felt directed to teach him what I had come to learn and help him comprehend the words pertaining to faith and its healing capabilities. Each day for eleven days, my regimen was the same: go to the hospital, read the Bible with Dad, and pray for his recovery. I knew if we had faith the size of a mustard seed we could remove the mountains in front of us.

One night, in my room, I felt the weight so greatly from walking through the valley of the shadow of death. All I could do alone in my room was cry out, "Oh, God! I am so helpless . . . so powerless! And I am nothing without you. My only hope is that you'll give us the grace to make it through. Please, give my dad encouragement and joy."

As we neared the end of our eleven dark days, I was sorely in need of encouragement and joy myself. I am so thankful to the Christian friends in Germany who showed us such kindness. Though we had never met them before, the brotherhood we shared in Jesus Christ caused them to treat us as one of them. One evening they even took me to a Saturday night worship service. I remember being mentally and physically exhausted, but I needed to be with others for their support and love. I sang praise songs in German and listened to the Word of God through an interpreter. The Holy Spirit is the same in any language, and without a doubt I left that night a renewed and encouraged man.

At the end of the eleven days, the doctors informed us that they could do nothing more to help Dad. The cancer was too far advanced, and yes, it had spread into his lungs. The news was sobering; and as they gave us drugs to be administered every single day for the rest of his life, I knew they were really giving up any hope of a recovery. They gave me instructions regarding the pills and injections, the latter of which I got the duty of giving. We packed our things and readied ourselves for the journey home.

Dad's phlebitis was so bad in his right leg I had to put one of my size 15 shoes on his size 11 foot. We dressed, packed our bags, and waited for one of our new friends to pick us up and take us to the airport. It was hard to believe we had come so far only to be sent home to continue combating the illness.

When the car arrived, I took Dad in my arms and carried him. Nearly forty years had passed since Dad carried me from a hospital room, bragging about how my life would someday fill his with pride. The tables had drastically turned.

Dad was still suffering a great deal of pain and was in very bad shape as I put him into the car. His eyes were dark, and almost all his strength was gone. His right foot began to swell even more. When we reached the airport I tried to remove the shoe I had put on his foot, but it wouldn't come off. As the odds of a smooth trip home began to mount against us, I could only petition God to go before us and give us the patience we needed as we made the long flight.

I asked for seats in the no smoking section, and we boarded a 747 for our trans-Atlantic flight. Once we were aboard, we discovered we had been assigned seats in a smoking section! I asked to be moved, but the jumbo jet was packed and there was no place to move. Dad could barely breathe as it was, and he would be subjected to cigarette smoke for ten hours. One thing was certain, however; despite the smoke I would get no protest from Dad. He was in such a weakened state, he couldn't talk or even raise his head.

I lifted the armrest between us and helped him get comfortable lying on both our seats. I stood in the back of the plane for most of the trip. Again, I prayed for patience. We made it.

For one whole month, the days and nights consisted of administering pills and three hundred drops of medication daily, as well as the injections. The nights were the most horrendous. As the pain increased, we had to resort to liquid morphine; but the morphine made him so sick he couldn't keep any food down.

No one really understand fully the uniqueness of my relationship with my father. Nearly every good memory I have includes his face and his words. When he laughed, I was happy. When he suffered through the hardships of coaching, I suffered. When Dad's heart was broken, so was mine. When he sacrificed his love and time for me, I wanted to give it back to him. Because of the years of closeness, I can truly say that whatever happened to him somehow happened to me. The pain of cancer is incredible and surely indescribable, but I can say I felt the pain as I watched my dad asking for morphine to ease it.

For several months I canceled all speaking engagements and public appearances to be by his side constantly. I dedicated myself to believing and praying with him. When I detected the slightest indication that he was thinking of giving up, I went to him with a reminder that God hadn't called anyone to give up.

We continued praying together, and eventually, Dad became comfortable. Not comfortable with the pain, but assured that if he lived or died his circumstances were in the hands of God and not his own. When bitterness could have had victory in the situation, Dad felt only love and gentleness.

On March 20, 1987, I walked into Dad's room to find him curled up in the bed like a baby in the womb. It was the third day in a row that he had refused food or drink, and his skin looked like it was falling off him, he was so dehydrated. We checked him back into the hospital where they immediately pumped his body full of nutrients and fluids to sustain him.

Something inexplicable happened that day as I stood near my father's bed. There he lay with tubes in his arms and tubes in his nose. I should have been depressed and despondent, but for the first time in weeks I felt a peace in my heart and mind like I'd never known during the whole situation. I was reminded of Psalm 112, "Unto the upright there arises light in the darkness."

It's amazing to me how many times people gave up on Dad during his illness. When his breathing was at 20 percent, I prayed for him. When I spent forty hours at a time by his bedside, I prayed and thanked God for him. When volunteers came in to sit with him during the dreadful nights of drug-induced hallucinations, we prayed for him.

As I watched my dad getting more sickly each day, I prayed for a miracle. As I prayed, I thought how great it would be to someday stand on a platform with my father, traveling the country and telling the world about Jesus Christ and how our hope lies in him. Then I realized the real miracle had already happened. The miracle is the amazing growth our relationship underwent because of our faith in Jesus. The illness drew us close, but the love we shared in Christ drew us closer than I ever believed possible.

I always knew that my Dad and I had a very special relationship; he was not only my father and coach, he was my friend and confidant. We shared the same dream, the same passion in life, but our dream had only brought us sorrow. All the fame and fortune the dream had promised left us as empty men until the day we received Jesus Christ into our hearts. At that point I became more than an heir to a dream, I became an heir to salvation and so did Dad.

God worked mightily in both our lives. For the last three years I had thought God was using me to teach Dad, but I found out it was just the opposite.

I learned a lot from my dad. Through his sickness he taught me that it's one thing to talk about the battle, and another thing to do battle. Dad faced the physical battle of cancer after a year and a half of being a Christian and his faith never waivered.

Dad used to hate everybody who had stabbed us in the back through the years, but now he didn't have one ounce of bitterness.

My father was a changed man for sure. When he was in our house fighting the cancer, he never cried out. He just prayed. When I looked in on him during the middle of the night, I would find him in the middle of saying a prayer. He had achieved such a peace with God in his life.

I sat with my father for hours on end, sometimes going two days without sleep. I'll never forget the day he looked up at me and said, "It seems like yesterday when I sat where you're sitting and my dad was lying here. He died in my arms, and I know I will die in yours. That comforts me."

In the midst of Dad's sickness and the turmoil it brought on us, we could experience peace; a peace I had sought my entire life.

On April 15, 1987, during the last five minutes of his life, I sat by his bed, holding his hand. I noticed a peacefulness in Dad's face like I'd never seen. The wrinkles in his forehead didn't seem to be there any longer. For about half an hour I had been sharing with him about the love of Jesus and the unspeakable joy we would experience when we saw him face to face.

I leaned over to whisper what would be my final words in his ear. "Dad, I want you to know that I will never give up. I will stand and believe until your last breath that God will heal you." I leaned closer, and said, "Someday I'll be with you. I love you."

As I sat there looking at the man I adored, God's loving and compassionate arm reached down to eternally heal Dad of any more pain and suffering.

There are no words to express the emptiness and pain I felt at that moment. At one time in my life I would have cursed God for the cancerous death of my father, but today I can thank him instead, because I know we'll be able to spend eternity together.

Afterword

Induction into the Basketball Hall of Fame is the "Oscar" of basketball achievement. Most who have received the high ordination make it a point to find their way back every year to Springfield, Massachusetts, to join the newcomers in the celebration of their election. This amazingly small brotherhood of honorees is bonded together by a common knowledge that out of the thousands who have given so much of their lives to Professor Naismith's game, only 161 have received the great honor.

Dad had often talked of the day I would be inducted into the Hall of Fame, and now I realize that was more his dream than mine. Sure, he would have loved it if I had fulfilled that other vision he gave me—winning a championship ring and being recognized as a member of the greatest team in the world. But my father had another notion in his mind and that was to see my entry into the Hall of Fame, with or without a championship.

These memories of Dad's goals for me were so clear on May 5, 1987, as I sat on a platform in Springfield, Massachusetts, surrounded by the most revered of all basketball achievers. Ironically, I once had told Dad back in my college days that if I ever made the Hall of Fame I would refuse the award and tell them they had given it to the wrong guy. "Give the award to my Dad," I had told him I'd say, "because there is no way in the world I deserve the honor before he does." My words from the past revisited me as I thought of what to say in my acceptance remarks.

I thought of the joy in Dad's face just three months ago when I told him the Hall of Fame had called announcing my selection. Through the pain of the cancer his eyes had lit up, and for a few moments the happiness relieved him of his suffering. I had looked into his loving eyes hoping he would survive long enough to share the important moment.

Now as I sat beside Rick Barry, Walt Frazier, and other great players about to be inducted, I remembered how Dad's countless hours of devotion to me and his commitment to helping me become one of the best had brought me to the Hall of Fame. I wished I could thank him for his devotion. I had a very hollow feeling as my father missed the day he had longed for.

Those in charge of the honors reminded us of the importance of the medallion we were about to receive. "The medallion will hang in the hall forever. It will hang there as a symbol of your accomplishments." My dad would have smiled then, finally, at the Hall of Fame, when they announced my name—his name—"Peter Maravich."

As I look back now I finally feel as though I understand my inheritance. Dad handed me something beautiful and precious, and I will always be indebted to him. He gave me his life full of instruction and encouragement. He gave me hope in hopeless situations and laughter in the face of grim circumstances. Dad gave me an example of discipline unequaled, dedication unmatched. He gave me the privilege of seeing an unwavering faith when the darkness of life and death surrounded him.

But, more than anything, my father became a symbol of what love and compassion can do in anyone's life, and I am happy to accept that love as his heir to a dream.

I began writing this book shortly before discovering my father had bone cancer. I never thought then that the book would end this way—my penning these final thoughts just days after his death.

For the rest of my time on this earth I will treasure the precious last few months I had with Dad. I believe they were months any son would desire to have with his father. As difficult as they were, they allowed me to share my deepest feelings and thoughts with him. And now I've shared them with you.

CAREER STATISTICS AND RECORDS SET BY PETE MARAVICH

HIGH SCHOOL

Daniels High	Most points scored	483
Needham-Broughton	Most points single season	735
	Best average (46 games)	32
N. Carolina All-Star Game, East vs. West	Most points scored	47*

COLLEGE
NCAA

Highest point average per game (season)	44.5*	1969–70
Highest point average per game (career)	44.2*	1968–70
Most points scored (season)	1381*	1969–70
Most points scored (career)	3667*	1969–70
Most field goals attempted (season)	1168*	1970
Most field goals made (season)	522*	1969–70
Most field goals attempted (career)	3166*	1968–70
Most field goals made (career)	1387*	1968–70
Most free throws attempted (3 yr. career)	1152*	1968–70
Most free throws made (3 yr. career)	893*	1968–70
Most free throw attempts (game)	31	1969
Most free throws made (game)	30*	1969
50 or more points in a game (season)	10*	1970
50 or more points in a game (career)	28*	1968–70

Best scoring average by a:

	YR	G	FG	FT	PT.	AVE
Sophomore	1968	26	432	274	1138	43.8*
Junior	1969	26	433	282	1148	44.2*
Senior	1970	31	522	337	1381	44.5*

SOUTHEASTERN CONFERENCE
SINGLE GAME

Points scored (LSU vs. Alabama)	69*	2–7–70
Field goal attempts	57*	1–29–68
	57*	2–7–70
Field goals made	26*	12–11–69
	26*	2–7–70
Free throw attempts (vs. Florida)	27*	2–12–69
Free throws made (vs. Florida)	22*	2–12–69

Career Highlights
SEASON

Free throw attempts	243*	1967–68
Free throws made	199*	1967–68
Points scored	851*	1969–70
Average per game	47.3*	1969–70
Field goal attempts	741*	1969–70
Field goals made	338*	1969–70

CONFERENCE CAREER

Points scored	2383*	1968–70
Field goal attempts	2110*	1968–70
Field goals made	917*	1968–70
Free throw attempts	754*	1968–70
Free throws made	549*	1968–70
Assists	257	1968–70

LSU

Assists (career)	425	1968–70
Assists (season)	192	1969–70

COLLEGE VARSITY TOTALS (3 seasons)

G	FG	FGA	PCT.	FT	FTA	PCT.	RB	A	PF	TP	AVE.
83	1387	3166	.438	893	1152	.775	528	423	250	3667	44.2

ALL TIME COLLEGE SCORERS

Player	School	Games	Seasons	Last Yr	Points
1. Pete Maravich	LSU	83	3	1970	3667
2. Freeman Williams	Portland State	106	4	1978	3249
3. Harry Kelly	Texas Southern	110	4	1983	3066
4. Oscar Robertson	Cincinnati	88	3	1960	2973
5. Alfredrick Hughes	Loyola (Illinois)	120	4	1985	2914
6. Elvin Hayes	Houston	93	3	1968	2884
7. Larry Bird	Indiana State	94	3	1979	2850
8. Otis Birdsong	Houston	116	4	1977	2832
9. Wayman Tisdale	Oklahoma	104	3	1985	2661
10. Michael Brooks	La Salle	111	4	1980	2628

NBA

Top ten: highest scoring average (10,000 pt. minimum)	24.2*	1971–80
Top ten: most points scored in one game (New Orleans vs. Knicks)	68*	1977
Top ten: most free throws made (New Orleans vs. Knicks) 26 attempts	23*	1975
Most free throw attempts in one quarter (Atlanta vs. Chicago) Tied Oscar Robertson & Stan McKenzie	16*	1973
Top 25 career scorers	15,948*	1971–80

NBA TOTALS

G	MIN.	FGM	FGA	PCT.	FTM	FTA	PCT.	REB.	AST.	P.F.	PTS.	AV.
658	24316	6187	14025	.441	3564	4344	.820	2747	3563	1865	15948	24.2

*Record still held in 1987

Player of Week No. 1

Hot-Shot!

Maravich Fires District High of 36 Points

(Note—Each Monday during the basketball season, The Press will make a "Player of the Week" award, recognizing college players for outstanding performances week-by-week. The award does not necessarily go for high scoring feats, as floor play, both defensive and offensive, is considered equally important.)

Point-a-minute Man!

That pretty much describes Capt. Pete "Press" Maravich. Davis-Elkins' one-man basketball team, who romps off with the first "Player of the Week" award for his sensational play the past week.

Many teams find it hard enough to score as many as 36 points in a game, but that's just what Maravich, former Aliquippa High player, did all on his own against Salem (W. Va.), Teachers last Saturday.

It was a new district one-game record, bettering the former mark of 34 held jointly by Mel Cratsley (Tech) and Bill Laughlin (W. J.).

"Press" flipped 16 field goals and four fouls to rack up his 36-point total, but it still wasn't enough to prevent D-E from dropping a 73-59 decision to Salem.

Maravich ranks with the leading point-getters in the nation. On a recent Eastern trip, he scored 27 points against Long Island U, and the next night collected 30 against La Salle—but D and E lost both games.

SENATORS LOSE TO SALEM COLLEGE SATURDAY NIGHT

Press Maravich Sets Scoring Mark With 36 Points

Salem Tigers Outscore Davis and Elkins 73 to 59

Salem college decisively defeated the Senators at Salem on Saturday night by a 73 to 59 count. But one Peter Maravich did all that one person could do to change the result.

Press was not "hot" in the true sense of the word, for he was not racking up his usual proportion of long shots, but he was playing his heart out to keep it a ball game. Thirty-six points was his record for the evening, and every one of the 36 was scored the hard way.

That Salem was laying for Maravich was evident. He was seldom if ever in the open and on only one occasion made a shot without having to sneak it under the arms of the tall Salem guards. Time and again the audience gasped to see Maravich execute seemingly impossible shots, but time and again he came back to flash under the defense of the Tigers and ring up another two pointer.

Maravich Is Offense

For two quarters, Press was the Senators' offense. A one point foul added by Mams as the second quarter began and a bucket by Setar were the only tallies made by the other four men on the squad. Maravich, in the meantime, was keeping D. and E. in the game. While it is true that he did not add point for point with the Ten Milers, he did put on a one-man scoring show that kept the Senators within 13 points of the Davismen all the way, and at times he rang up scores enough to pull the Senators to within six points of the always-leading Tigers. . . .

VARSITY LOSES BY 89-77

Pistol Pete & Playmates Overflow Coliseum, Rout Rebs, 110 to 98

By DAN HARDESTY
State-Times Sports Editor

Home basketball action has ended at LSU for another season, but not before Pete Maravich and Company filled the house.

They finally had to close the front doors of the Coliseum last Saturday night because there wasn't room for any more spectators inside. And with the big barn jammed to its capacity of 8,500, the Tiger freshmen outscored a strong Ole Miss frosh club, 110 to 98.

Then, after about 3,000 of the fans had gone home, the Tiger varsity tackled the Ole Miss varsity. The result was the 21st defeat of the season for LSU, with almost all of the fans gone by the time the final whistle sounded with the scoreboard showing 89 to 77 for the visitors.

The Rebs hit a red hot .594 from the floor in the first half and after a close start, they pulled out to a 52-42 halftime edge. LSU never was able to catch up, even though the Rebels did cool off considerably in their shooting.

Ole Miss hit 50 per cent of its field goals for the entire game, and LSU 40 per cent. The Tigers didn't do much better from the foul line, hitting only 13 of 23, while Ole Miss was dropping in one after another, 31 of 35 in all.

Brad Brian led Tiger scorers with 19 points and Larry Martindale of the Rebs had the same number.

In posting their 17th straight victory, the Tiger freshman team ran into some of its strongest opposition of the year. Ole Miss stayed right with them—and ahead of them for quite a while—and the overflow crowd got a lot of action in the home finale.

Pete Maravich, although having one of his poorest shooting nights of the season, scored 45 points, almost exactly his season average. He hit only 14 of 41 field goal attempts, with about a dozen rolling off the rim. He sank 17 of 21 free throws.

(from the **Baton Rouge State-Times**)

BUT TIGS LOSE, 74-69

Maravich Cracks Season
Scoring Record in SEC

By SAM KING
State-Times Sports Writer

AUBURN, Ala.—What'll he do for an encore?
Pistol Pete Maravich, LSU's saggy-socked sophomore sensation, shot down his second major Southeastern Conference record of the season here Wednesday night as he eclipsed the single season scoring mark held by Bob Pettit and still has eight more games to add to this mark.

It was a spectacular second-half performance which lifted the skinny-legged "shotsation" over the 785-point standard set by Pettit when he played for LSU in 1954. Maravich practially had the partisan Auburn fans standing on their heads in the second half when he scored 25 straight points for LSU and wound up with 31 of the Tigers 37 during the final 20 minutes of play.

His 49-point output for the game shoved his point total for the season to 793, but even this wasn't enough to turn back Auburn, which came out on top, 74-69. The Tigers, outrebounded 51-26, have now suffered five consecutive setbacks and face still another tough obstacle, Florida, come Saturday afternoon at the Ag Coliseum at LSU.

The Tigers will carry a 10-8 over-all mark into the Gator game, which will be telecast and for the first time this year, the Bengals will be entering a game below the .500 mark in SEC play with a 5-6 showing.

Maravich, who claimed the SEC single-game scoring record with a 58-point performance against Mississippi State earlier in the year, worked his way around, through and over Auburn for 47 attempts—several in a bid to draw fouls—and connected on 18 two-pointers. He had a flawless night at the free throw line bucketing 13 of 13.

Maravich tied Pettit's 785-point record with 7:58 left in the half. He eclipsed the mark at 7:39 with a 20-foot jump shot from the left side of the key.

The record-breaking bucket came on the tail end of a streak of eight points by the Bengal sharp-shooter in a mite over a minute, which rallied the Tigs from 11 behind to five of Auburn. The record-breaking shot also was the 24th and 25th straight points in a row for the Tigs since the start of the second half.

The first Bengal bucket by anyone other than Pete in the second half came at 6:57 when Ralph Jukkola, who wound up the night with 12 markers, hit a layup following a steal by hustling Rich Lupcho. Jukkola hit another layup and sank both ends of a one-and-one before the game ended for the only other points made in the second half other than those by Maravich.

Maravich is rapidly nearing the national mark set by Frank Selvy of Furman in 1954 when he sported a 41.7 mark in 29 games for the NCAA mark. Pete needs to average 36 a game to top that mark, but beating Selvy's total point output may take some doing, as he had 1,209 and played in three more games than Pete will play this season. . . .

(from the **Baton Rouge State-Times**)

RALIEGH ROUNDBALLING

Pete's Best, Smith's Spurt
Nail Enloe to League Cellar

By BOB WILLS
Times Sports Writer

Broughton's amazing Pete Maravich put on quite a show, but it was a 13-point spurt by carrot-top senior Dickie Smith in the final three minutes of play that nailed Enloe with an 83-71 loss and toppled the Eagles back into the cellar of the Eastern 4-A scrappings here last night.

Maravich, popping 'em in from downtown and from almost unbelievable positions, stripped the nets for 47 points, his career high, but when it came down to the wire Smith cracked it open with ease.

"It was Maravich all the way up until the end and then Smith took over," said Eagle boss Howard Hurt, seemingly in a state of semi-shock at the finale. "We got Broughton down by five and it looked as though we were going to break it open. Then Maravich went to work again."

The victory evened the Eagle-Cap series at 1-1 and was Broughton's third triumph in nine games. Enloe is 2-7 for the campaign, and now shares the bottom of the loop ladder with Wilson.

"Too much Maravich," continued Hurt. "We tried to defend him, but he just stood out there and threw it up. Most of them went in. The only way to defend him is to keep the ball out of his hands."

Maravich, 6-4 and 150 pounds, hit 18 of 28 from the floor and 11 of 12 from the foul line. It was the fourth time this year he scored 40 points or better.

With Maravich picking up only three points in the first quarter, Enloe behind a balanced attack, forged into a 17-14 lead. Despite 13 straight points by the Broughton ace in the second period, the Eagles managed to cling to a four-point cushion at the half, 35-31.

Maravich opened the third quarter with a strike from outside and closed it with a hit from the corner, but the hosts still led by three, 56-53.

Within a minute and a half of the fourth frame, the hothanded transfer from Clemson High of South Carolina, dumped in two field goals and four free throws to push the Caps into the lead, 61-60.

Two more free throws by Maravich with 5:06 to play gave Broughton the lead for good, 66-65. . . .

(from the **Raleigh Times**)

Maravich legend enjoying rebirth
by Gil LeBreton

Dallas—Pistol Pete. That wasn't just a nickname. That was a basketball state of mind.

It was floppy socks. Between-the-legs dribbles. Between-the-legs passes. Showtime. Swish. Forty-four points swishing through, game-after-game, every game, for three collegiate seasons.

The name that launched a thousand shots. OK, make that 3,166 shots.

Pistol Pete Maravich didn't just play basketball. He spray-painted it, just so we'd all remember.

"Maravich? Pistol Pete?" the hotel operator chirped Friday. "Oooh, is he staying here, too?"

So you see, Earvin Johnson, with all due respect, this dude was making magic while you were still making mud pies.

Likewise, with all due respect to Julius Erving, Maravich was anesthetizing basketball minds when the kind doctor was still changing bedpans.

How appropriate Pistol Pete should join us this weekend for a gathering of National Basketball Association legends. His pro career never reached the heights that his seasons at Louisiana State did, but Maravich did get picked for five NBA All-Star games.

And how ironic that Pete Maravich, who touched millions during his college years, wonders these days why, playing a different role, he can't touch a few more.

That's the Pete Maravich story now. You watched, so now he'd like you to listen. You put a spotlight on him, so now he'd like to show you the light.

"Money didn't change me," Maravich said Friday, on the eve of the NBA Legends Classic. "Money didn't change me, or power, or fame, or All-Star games or being Pistol Pete. Those were only brief interludes of ego gratification.

"The only thing that ever changed me was Jesus Christ. . . ."

231

Maravich's coaching just part of his gifts to SEC basketball

by John Adams

Press Maravich did not win as many games as he lost as an LSU basketball coach. And after six years, he had not won enough games to keep his job.

He later had three losing seasons at Appalachian State. He then became a scout for the New Orleans Jazz.

He did not leave us a Hall-of Fame resume. But he did far more for college basketball in Louisiana and the Southeast than many coaches who won more games.

Press Maravich, 71, was buried in Aliquippa, Pa., yesterday. Unless he had a change of heart in his later years, there was a basketball beside him in the coffin. The game meant that much to him, he once said.

The name Maravich meant little to me when I enrolled at LSU as a freshman journalism student. I knew he was a new basketball coach at a school where home games sometimes were moved to a high school gym, so the Agriculture Coliseum could accommodate something important, like a rodeo. I knew he was sure to have a losing season.

A week before the first game, a friend in the dormitory told me about another Maravich, the coach's son. "You're not going to believe this guy," Billy told me. "You're not going to believe what he can do with a basketball."

The guy I didn't believe was Billy.

Nonetheless, I went to the first freshman basketball game. And like almost everybody else in attendance, I went to the next one, too. And the next.

Billy was right. I realized that after three minutes of watching "Pistol Pete" Maravich dribble the ball behind his back, between his legs and between the legs of the man guarding him.

I had never seen anybody like him on a basketball court. I still haven't.

From 1966 to 1970, I watched Maravich dribble, pass and shoot from angles and distances that drew raves and sighs. He set a national scoring record and produced as many oohs and aahs as he did points.

LSU games became sellouts. Students spent the night in front of the coliseum doors to assure themselves of a choice seat for an afternoon game against Kentucky. Because the coliseum could not accommodate an entire city, the games were taped and replayed at 10:30 p.m. on a local television station.

The fascination with Maravich extended to every SEC campus. Suddenly, Kentucky was not the only act worth seeing.

Pete would have been a star at any school, under any coach. But he would not have been Pistol Pete. He would not have been the most entertaining college basketball player of all time.

Press did not hesitate showcasing his son. He gave him the basketball, center stage and just enough props.

Together, they never had a losing season. They became a cover story in a conference whose headlines traditionally were stripped above a Lexington, Ky., dateline.

In Pete's senior season, LSU was 22-10 and advanced to the semifinals of the National Invitation Tournament.

Two years later, Press was fired. And after three ignominious seasons at Appalachian State, he was out of coaching.

Yet under different circumstances, Press Maravich might have become entrenched as LSU's basketball coach. Had he been allowed to recruit black players when he was hired, he might have had a talent base that would have sustained the momentum his son started.

Press was beset with problems at home during his years at LSU. His wife, who was chronically ill, killed herself in 1974. During her illness, Press had to run a household (with a young daughter) and a basketball team.

The problems did not affect his coaching, according to his former assistant, Jay McCreary. "He was a hell of a coach," McCreary said. "And I think I was in a better position to judge than anybody. . . ."

Are the Celtics Happy Ending for the Pistol?

"If I'm fortunate enough to be on the team that wins it this year . . . At least I want them to know that I share it with (New Orleans)."
—Pete Maravich

By JIMMY SMITH
(Times-Picayune Sports Writer)

BOSTON—He continues his 10-year chase of the dream that eludes him. Yet as he pulls on his green-trimmed Boston Celtics jersey, there is a feeling of quiet confidence, the promise of a happy ending.

For the first time in his life, Pete Maravich sees the glimmer of the golden pot at the end of the rainbow. No team in the National Basketball has traversed the multi-colored path more successfully than the Celtics.

Thirteen world championship banners hang majestically over the floor of the Boston Garden here as the Celts, led by their leprechaun mascot and seemingly unending talent, have dominated the NBA as no other team ever has.

The fact is not lost on the one known as The Pistol.

"I think day in and day out about pouring champagne on Red Auerbach's head," Pete says softly, sitting in front on his locker in the Celtics's dressing room. "I never was in this game for personal pleasure. I was only in it this long because of one thing. That's the championship that has eluded my reach. It's always been a frustrating thing for me."

Starting his career with the Atlanta Hawks, Maravich appeared in the playoffs three times but never reached the finals. For five years he struggled to make the New Orleans Jazz a contender, but, he was a one-man show. He didn't play in Utah, saying the situation is "not worth talking about."

So when Utah cut him loose, he was free to make his own deal. The Celtics were interested, as was their Atlantic Conference rival Philadelphia.

All his life, though, Maravich wanted to wear Celtic green.

"This is the place I've always wanted to be," he says, passing his hand through his boyish-looking, newly-curled hair. "I think any player always wants to be a Celtic. They're the ones with all the championships. Beantown is known for basketball."

And all his life, the Pistol has wanted one reward for his efforts—a championship ring. Playing a reserve role off the bench for the Celtics—currently the best team in basketball—Maravich realizes he'll never have a better shot at realizing his dream. Above all, he's happy with the role he's playing.

"This is my shot," he says, adjusting an ice pack on his right knee. "It's a pleasureable experience now. It really is. Larry (Bird) is going through exactly the same thing I went through. I enjoy it now. All I care about doing is contributing and being a part of something that wins it. . . ."

(from the **New Orleans Times-Picayune**)

'Pistol Pete' to enter Hall

From staff and wire reports

Pistol Pete Maravich, college basketball's Division I career scoring leader, was elected to the Basketball Hall of Fame on Thursday.

Maravich, who starred at LSU and later played in the National Basketball Association with the Atlanta Hawks, New Orleans-Utah Jazz and Boston Celtics, was elected along with Rick Barry, Walt Frazier, Bob Houbregs and Bobby Wanzer.

Frazier, an All-Star guard for the New York Knicks, witnessed two of Maravich's most memorable performances. On Oct. 26, 1975, Maravich scored 45 points in a double-overtime victory by the Jazz over the Knicks. Frazier, known for his defensive prowess, was guarding Maravich.

On Feb. 25, 1977, Maravich scored 68 points against the Knicks in a 124-107 victory by the Jazz.

Houbregs was the 1953 NCAA Player of the Year, and Wanzer was a six-time All-Star with the former Rochester Royals of the NBA.

Maravich brought interest in basketball to the South, generally a one-sport (football) region, in the late 1960s at LSU with dazzling ball-handling and prolific scoring. Maravich scored 3,667 points—the NCAA Division I record—and had a career average of 44.2 points.

He once scored 52 points in a game, but had the audience talking more about an assist. Maravich, on a two-on-one break, hit the outside man for a layup with a left-handed (he was right-handed) behind-the-back pass. "My God," cried Carl Stewart, then the coach of predominantly black Southern University, "he's one of us!"

In Maravich's 68-point performance against the Knicks, he made 26 of 43 field-goal attempts. Scoring 17, 14, 17 and 20 points in each quarter, Maravich fouled out with 1:18 to play on two questionable calls.

One basket was erased when it was ruled he stepped out of bounds. A sequence of photographs later showed Maravich was forced out by Butch Beard, meaning New Orleans should have at least retained possession. Then, Maravich fouled out on a hairline charging call while making a field goal. "Another ref," Maravich said wearily, "and it could have been a three-point play."

It was the only game Maravich fouled out of during the 1976-77 season.

Maravich led the NBA in scoring in 1976-77 (31.1) and was a four-time NBA All-Star.

The five will be inducted during ceremonies May 5 at the Springfield (Mass.) Civic Center, increasing the Hall of Fame's roster to 161. Nominees must receive 18 votes from a 24-member Honors Committee to be chosen. . . .